THE WHISPERING WILLOWS

LEONI ROBENS

Powered by

24by7Publishing.com

This book **'The Whispering Willows'** by Leoni Robens
is self-published by the author.

All the printing & distribution process of the book is powered by

24by7 Publishing
13 New Road, Kolkata - 51, India
https://www.24by7publishing.com
mail@24by7publishing.com
+91 9831 470 133
+91 9433 444 334

MRP: INR 445.00

First Published in March, 2024

Version 1.00

ISBN: 978-81-969169-4-7

Powered by

24by7Publishing.com

Dedication

Wayfarers all!
Invited to the Mr Toad's
Dooliyaanah Mansion
All aunts, uncles, cousins
Grandpa's, grandma's
Nieces, nephews
Sisters and brothers
Hear Ye and Spare Ye
A precious moment
To read my book
The funny adventures
Of Mr Toady and his friends
Mr Moley, Mr Badger and Mr Water Ratty
The otter, foxes, weasels, stoats
Badgers, hares, rabbits
Hedgehogs, porcupines
Ferrets, gerbils, vixen
Cats, dogs, lizards
Cocks, geese, mice
Ducks and drakes
Horses and lambs
Their bitter or sweet tails
Left behind
Till they come home happy again

As she typed
Sofie her Faery tale
The Little Bo Peep of the century
To have and behold
The retold story
Of the Wind In the Willows
By Kenneth Grahame
Transformed into the
Whispering Willows
"ARAVAH YASHUWA
SONG IACHASHU!"
To men whisper Willows
To Jesus my splendid retelling
(In Hebrew)

About the Author

The author goes by the nom de plume Leoni Robens, loves writing poems of love, valour, knights in shining armour, giants, mermaids and all sorts of fairy folks. She has won a scholarship in English and won certificates for elocution, drama, singing and handwriting. The author loves cooking, gardening, painting and singing and has sung in her mother-in-law, Heather's choir for many shows performed on stage. Her favourite authors are George MacDonald, William Shakespeare, Lewis Carroll, Enid Blyton, Frances Hodgson Burnett and Hans Christian Andersen and her favourite book is Alice in Wonderland. She completed her Bachelor's degree in Commerce. At present she is a housewife, but still continues writing these enjoyable poems, to entertain adults as well as young minds with some fun and magic. She believes that the "PEN IS MIGHTIER THAN THE SWORD" and hopes that one day her pen will bring out the best in song, dance and dramatics to be performed on stage by budding enthusiastic young actors, which would add another feather to her cape.

She lives in Mumbai with her husband, son, mother and adorable pet African Grey Parrot Romeo, as well as charming Moustached Parakeets, Charlie Brown and Alice Liddle.

Her published books- "A Fairy's Quill: Poetry Book for Children", "Maguk World- Wonderland Fairy Carousel of Poems", "The Maguk

Well" & "MAGIC COMPOSITIONS! Stories reflecting sea creatures and sprites of the earth!" are quite popular among young readers. This one "THE WHISPERING WILLOWS" based on the Wind in the Willows by Kenneth Grahame surely will not disappoint her readers. Happy Reading into the marvellous land of Mr Toady and his friends unforgettable adventures of the Wild Wood Yonder!

INTRODUCTION

TEARS LIKE SUMMER'S TEMPEST!

Tales like stories of the Wind in the Willows have secrets of trees like Willows of mystical symbolism. Different types of trees have their own meaning, depending where they grow and tales have been woven around them over the years. The wild wood creatures living in the wild woods have so many of the alluring whispering willows, often symbolising flexibility and adaptability. The timber and supple nature of its extremities means it bends to accommodate and withstand strong winds and adverse weather like the cycles in our life span, sometimes blowing mellow and sometimes huffing strong...happy rumours or throwing jibes at us, just like whispers of a faery Willow. Not meaning to be harsh but teaching its lessons just like the cycle of life- birth, growth, regeneration and death ultimately.

Mr Toad along with his friends Mr Water Ratty, Mr Moley, Mr Otter and Mr Badger show us, how true friendship is unshakable and its foundation so deep like its sustaining roots- powerful, nourishing and so strong that binds us with consolation of facing the most difficult and most terrifying challenges, also sharing moments of sweetness and tranquillity. Overcoming all our temptations, vices and using our talents and usefulness to help our family and also to bring out our fruits of labour into sprawling branches of ambition, for others to share, enjoy and spread the meaning of Whispering Willows

Aptly said the tree and its long life-the appearance as if it were weeping, Psalm 137 states; "There on the willow trees, we hung up our harps" The verse is written from the perspective of Jews who were being held captive in Babylon and are fondly remembering their homeland. Here the willow tree symbol represents both loss and hope.

The weeping willows are also associated with grief and mourning, it's common to find weeping willow trees in graveyards in Asian countries, particularly China. And features in Asian folk tales and art depicting loss and mourning. As well they were often carried around or placed at doorways to keep evil spirits away. Whilst in many European folklores particularly Celtic and Druid beliefs, the famous phrase "Knock on wood", is believed came from Willow Trees, people believed willow trees brought good luck, and they would knock on its trunk to bring good fortune.

Another reference to the willow tree is made in Ezekiel 17:5 The Prophet plants a seed and "Sets it like a willow tree" This makes the Symbol of Willow of rebirth and vitality, even the "Willows of the Brook" Leviticus 23:40, where willow is portrayed as celebratory, with believers being told to offer a willow sprig or branch as a custom or tradition. According to Native Americans who have a strong connection to nature, the willow tree is often said to bring good luck and protect them from bad weather and to their homes to protect the Great Spirit.

The sound of the wind blowing through a willow tree's leaves was also said to be elves whispering to one another. In ancient Greek Mythology, Orpheus, the bringer of song, carried willow wood with him to protect against evil in the underworld. Hecate, the malevolent Goddess of witchcraft, also used a wand made of willow. Willow is connected to song, dancing and music, even the harp that Apollo gifted Orpheus was made of willow wood.

Last but not the least Willow Tree symbolism in literature and pop culture cannot go unnoticed, A Ubiquitous tree, the willow has been cited and written about in cultural works from Desdemona's "Willow Song", in Shakespeare's Othello to the sprite "Grandmother Willow" in Pocahonthas and the "Whomping Willow" in Harry Potter. My book the Whispering Willow symbolises love, loss, wisdom and power of friendship by the unforgettable story of Classic Wind in the Willows!

Concluding that the Willow Tree till today is a wondrous way to help us feel connected with our ancestors, as well as the cultures around the world. Realizing that for thousands of years, people looked at it the same way to connect with it with same emotions of love and loss that makes us feel connected to our fellow humans now and then. In this way, it's not only the longevity of a single willow tree

But the permanence of the willow trees in our world, that serve as a reminder of endurance and perpetuity. Happy reading, Dear Folks! My faery book **"The Whispering Willows by Leoni Robens" May you cry tears so big, joyous and unpredictable like Tears of a Summers Tempest!**

A TAIL OF TALES OF RATTY, BADGER, MOLEY AND TOAD

THE LITTLE BO-PEEP OF THE CENTURY SUMS UP!

Little Bo-Peep

Little Bo-Peep has lost her sheep,
And can't tell where to find them;
Leave them alone, and they'll come home,
Bringing their tails behind them.

Little Bo-Peep fell fast asleep,
And dreamt she heard them bleating;
But when she awoke, she found it a joke,
For they were still all fleeting.

Then up she took her little crook,
Determined for to find them;
She found them indeed, but it made her heart bleed,
For they'd left their tails behind them.

It happened one day, as Bo-Peep did stray
Into a meadow hard by,
There she espied their tails, side by side,
All hung on a tree to dry.

She heaved a sigh and wiped her eye,
And over the hillocks she raced;
And tried what she could, as a shepherdess should,
That each tail be properly placed.
The tales of Moley, Badger, Water Ratty, Otter

And of course Toad her friends,
Their enlightened lamp lights and tails
Happily home at last, to last till eternity or EWIGKEITH!
A twinkle brat Bartholomew Price of an Oxford Don teacher of Lewis Carol
That inspired the Twinkle Batty Brat song, here inspired me my brat
Mad hatter husband Johann and tweets to my handsome son Brett
A Twinkle song so our lights of imagination never die down!
TWINKLE BRAT SONG!

Twinkle Twinkle little brat
How I wonder what your hat?
Up above the world so high
Like a timeless tea pot you shy
And now you pour your dazzle pot
With stars that never grow old nor die
But remain your mummy's star
Forever till she stones like char
And melts into the brew of sky
A tea tray full of your shining diamonds
Twinkle Twinkle little brat
Now my son I know what spells your cat!
Scratch the surface
And you'll find those rare rough diamonds
Called Brats up in the skies!
When the blazing sun is gone
Nothing else shines upon
You show your light
All the night
Like a traveller in the dark
Thanks my son and husband for your tiny spark

He could not see which way to go
If you did not twinkle so
Remember mummy will guide you know
When the path seems rough to tarry
In the dark blue skies you keep
And oft' through my curtains peep
For you never shut your eye
Till the sun is in the sky
'Ts your bright and tiny spark
Lights the traveller in the dark
Though I know what you are
You are my brave knight of a son
And knave of a dashing husband
Who overcomes every woe
And sets my night with the brightest
Diadem known to be my precious
Diamonds!
Twinkle brightly and shine my precious
Like a Brat forever till the kettle
Pours out magic and makes your every dream turn true!
Like a portal tea tray portent that opens every once a while
A pleasant whispering willow time!
To my readers and the stars above that shine!
Leoni Robens

THE WHISPERING WILLOWS

Sofie's troubles had landed her in a soup
Reading through her large rimmed spectacles
Almost as big as Sophie herself
She decided to start penning a novel
Based on true characters
On the beautiful story of the Wind in The Willows
Written by Kenneth Grahame
Only this time the characters of the story book
Would be her dearest Uncles, Aunts
Grandmother and Grandfather
Cousins and acquaintances
With fortitude built like a pack of cards
Or Jenga a ton of bricks
Laying it layer by layer, brick by brick
Into a stupendous story book for keeps
Named the Whispering Willows

Characters of the wild wood
Mole- Molly or Joanna
Water Ratty- Joe or Joseph
Badger- Johnny or John
Toady- As Charming Mr Toad
Dotty Grimmwauld- As Toadess Dotty Grimmwauld

Great Great Great Grand Uncle Mr Dooliyaanah Little Toad - As Uncle Donny

Kindly old Weasel- Mary

Also as Grandmother Ferret Mary Rose Magdalene Herbage

Horse- Davidson or David

Also as Grandfather Ferret Michael Devasia Mathai Herbage

Bunny Rabbit- Leoni

Also as a Ballet High Ballerina of Mist and Dew

The great African Grey- Romeo

Moustache Parakeets- Charlie Brown and Alice Liddle

Golden haired faery Ferret- Jill

March Hare- Theresa

Also as the Golden Dinner Bell Faery Tinkerbelle

Beaver Mr Nuttle- Chef of Mr Toad

Tommy the young otter- Jolene

Lizard Police Watch Guard- Christopher

Well mannered Stoat- Donita

Mrs Badger- Philo

Hedgehog brothers:

Hedgehog little- Denzil

Hedgehog great- Daniel

Gerbilly Master of Christmas choir- Mr Brett

Choir of Church Meeces- His Cousins

The Prison Warden or Gaoler, A wild ferret- Paul

The stout Badger Washer Woman- Lydia

The Train Driver Mr Pussycat Handlebars- Johann

Strict Rooster Kindergarten Teacher or Principal- Lenny

Gypsy Beaver- Stephen

Princess Cleoratra- Tulip

Foxes- The enemies

Otter- Anonymous

Police officer Stoats, Meeces and the Hound Baskerville Sergeant of Police

Owl of Judges and Stork, Pelicans, Herons

Quails and Flamingoes-Members of the trusted jury

Sofie, began rat-a-tat-a-tat-a-tat
Pounding away at the keys of the typewriter
To start off with her poem
She often found writers block
And so many troubles
Like immense boulders writers often faced
Blundering her path
To turn them into her building blocks

SOFIE'S TROUBLES

Whether Sofie's pumpkin's patch
Would be full of turnips or radishes
Or rabbits, turtle doves, cocks and weasels
With a pumpkin head scarecrow and talking
Crunchy carrots
Purple lady Aubergines whisper to lady fingers
All about the plot of the charming
Animals down the lanes of the
Whispering willows
The jungle of garden friends Jamboree

SPRING CLEANING

Mr Mole had a lot of spring cleaning to do
Thick drops of paint fell on his white
Plastered face he covered with soft white muslin
To prevent from being totally white washed
As he wished to do a white washing chore
Around his old crusty walls
Deep down the hole in the mossy
Forest grounds
Beside the tall welcoming branches and sprawling roots
Of the whispering willows
He was at it the whole day
Haply brushing strokes
As paint brush would suffice
On a bare canvas
Upon the easel built of stone and rock
Down many miles under the turf
When looking up welcomingly at the ancient clock
Tick Tock Tick
It was time for a sip of coffee
Black and smug like the musty
Rooms he was so tired of being in day in and out
So decided the mole
"After I make a strong black Cherokee
Coffee as black as Black Ratty

The colour of his sleek velvety hair
Like a brush of black night sky
I shall climb out of my hole
And uppity into the clear
Sky blue atmosphere
Away from Spring Cleaning
And White Washing"
Then taking sips of a mug
Of hot piping brew
'Drink hot coffee Drink hot tea
Burn your lips and remember me!'
Played on his lips
As he sipped deliciously and finished
He soon started to dig upwards
The deep hole and into the blue marvellous sky tother end
To reach the ancient rat house of the Water Rat
It seemed after all their years of adventures
They had turned out to be best friends
As thick as thieves
Love thicker than Blood
Not to say Blood thicker than water
They exhorted to themselves
Criminals of an underground kingdom
The animals of the garden patch
Were almost from the same families
Of beloved rodents

As well as Badger who always
Was content with his own company
Reading most of the time like a book worm
With little time to spare
For three musketeers to gallivant
Their high horses
One special beloved friend the old buggy horse
Of Rich Mr Toady
They loved the little fellow David
And fed him with all they could afford
Barley sugar, corn and oats
In fact they loved befriending all Mr Toady's
Priceless beasts
Even his cocks, hens, bulls and rabbits
Squirrels, march hares, lizards,
Stoats, bumble bees, weasels,
Cats, dogs, beavers, shrews and voles
All who lived around the Whispering Willow garden
The critters of the Jamboree

As Mr Moley exited out through
The brilliant sunshine air
"ONION SAUCE! ONION SAUCE!"
He commented in tears, Moley to himself
Pleasingly swallowing in air and fresh oxygen molecules
Exhaling and breathing out carbon dioxide

In response the jungle exhaled thick mists
And dense clouds of vapour into a light fleeting drizzle
An exchange of airy fairy tête-à-tête
Rendezvous with nature!
When a large Alice Bunny Rabbit
Hopped close by
With a ticket in his hand
As if he were collecting a fare
For an adventure through the garden thicket
Surrounding the large wooded mansion of Mr Toady
Around a large river
They naturally would have to cross it
With a scull boat to reach it
This Water Ratty often did as a sport
With Mr. Mole and sometime Mr Badger
If he was available of course on their threesome
Adventures to Mr Toady's spiffy and natty
Spruce Mansion and wading through his spic lawns
There he saw a bright shining face
Though black his whiskers polished silvery
Like moonshine through the green foliage
Mr Ratty as if he wore a Black Velvet Two Tuxedo Tails
Was sitting on his blue and white Quadruple scull boat
With four pair of sculls or oars on either side
For Moley, Badger, Water Ratty and Toady of course
Who oft' missed their scull boating expeditions

A funny observation
The 'HAGGLE-POT' for bargaining about Picnic
Time to be spent fruitfully, choosing work over leisure
Or playtime over work
"All work and no play make Jack a dull boy"
He seemed embroiled in wheel play at helms
Explains that there's also a time and place
For old school haggling
Both parties chest their cards, each hoping
The other will misplay his hand
After lots of back and forth posturing
They settle on a fair and square price
On a Quad scull boating adventure of a Picnic Time
Each can live with
Although both know that the deal is likely
Better for one side than the other
"At some point, it still comes
Down to determining who gets which
Slice of the Pie"
The Cost price they'd haggle for!
The cost whether be relevant or irrelevant
Of Toady's guilty pleasures and joust car rides
Or the price they'd pay owing Toady's
Ambitious car racing sprees
When time against tide could be spent
Rowing, picnicking and fishing

Toady would miss his slice
Good from far, Far from better
By far getting himself into trouble again
For his misadventures
Once more they'd need to save him in the bargain!
But for now they had a taste of it all
Boating, fishing, fun and frolicking
Of their strange little HAGGLE-POT!

Ratty had just used his painter to fetch
From a deep hole right at the bottom
Where he lived a huge picnic basket
The hook he neatly burrowed inside the handles
Then bringing it up from the hole
Into his quad shell scull boat
Meant for four rowers and
Settled it just at the bottom of his feet
Staggering with its heavy tonnage
Panting whilst carrying the heavy weight of the picnic basket
"PUFF POOFF...PFFFF"
And finally dropping it down
Quiet excitedly jerking and tugging now
At the oar handles and calling out
"Moley Moley"
"Come fast let's sail our way through
The river brushes, bull rushes

And whispering willows
Looks like the occupants
Storks, ducks, song sparrows
Swansong entourage with necks
Humming birds, drakes, otters
Herons, little Egrets, Grebes
Kingfishers, Sandpipers, Lapwing
Gulls, flamingos, Swallows, Spoonbill
Cormorants and Mallards
Have filled its edges and hems
Let's cast away our sails
With fishing hooks and tackles
And hope to catch a few sole
And monk fishes in our baskets
Hook, line and sinker
With our drawly trawly crawly worm baits"
Mr. Mole quiet ecstatically exclaimed
"And what a steal
A whole basket of picnic surprises
I hope we find Mr Badger along the way
He would be surely surprised
As much as an owl or a pussy
It's good to poke the bear
Once in a while from his sleep"

The experienced water rat stroked

The silvery morning sunshine stars
That gleamed on the surface of the water
And made a quick brush through the placid stream
As the bull's rushes, tall ferns, the curious peeking flowers
Dragon flies, butterflies and lily pads kissed the edges of the boat
As it swayed through the ruffles of its
Rippling watery rings
Laughing and giggling out madly
In concentric circles around their scull boat
On the stern end sat Mr Mole
Enjoying their sail boating adventure
Hoping to catch up with lazy Mr Badger
Who lived just around the corner
In a very solemn hole
Somewhere deep down
The magical flora and fauna
They had a special bugle horn
They blew thrice in order to make notice
They arrived near his dwelling
Sometimes Water Ratty even whistled
As lovely as a pied pipe
Three encouraging notes
"Pheeeeeee Phepppehhheee Pheeeee Pheppehhhee"
To call and wake up Mr Badger from his
Day dreaming or sleepy snores

Luckily this time Mr Badger awoke
From his afternoon siesta
In just a second hoot on the strange
Bugle horn
And soon they saw a tan brown
Silvery grey head peeping
Up through the sign post below a little badger hole
His address mentioned clearly

‘MR BADGER DOWN HERE TRESPASSERS NOT ALLOWED’

Just a way to keep off those sly foxes
On their way to trick someone
Or maybe a prey for their empty stomachs
Which were always ravenously hungry
For maybe a mouthful not sparing
Even a kind soul
As Mr Moley, Mr Ratty, Mr Badger or Mr Toady
The heroes of our story
Thence they always advised never
To go at night through the horrid forest
Which at daytime didn’t seem at all so threatening
Or foreboding
To the innocent dwellers of the Whispering Willows

THE PICNIC

Mr Moley inspired and brainwashed
By the breathtaking splendour of early dawn
As the mist and fog uplifted the curtain
Of the dark mystery night
And the twinkle of stars died down
Unfurling wispy young morning smoky haze as if in a blessed daydream
The chatter and chortle of the birds and the buzzing of bees
Even translucent neon butterflies fluttering
Hither, thither and yon
Amongst the lush countryside
For he would so love to paint its surreal dream landscape
Upon an easel
Its innocent white illustrious canvas
As he always dabbled with paints
Even while spring cleaning or white washing
All the house, laundry and even himself
Now was filled with curiosity
What contained inside the heavy Luncheon basket
That was beneath Mr Water Ratty's feet
As Mr Water Ratty commented
Debating the unmistakable beauty
"Marvellous Marvellous
Such a picturesque landscape

Our water boat sails
Like a dream yonder blue horizon
It's myriad of little row houses
Like tiny attaché cases"
As they traversed inside the scull boat
Each with their oars
Even Mr Badger had carried his special
Four books, being an avid reader
The Maguk Well
The Fairy's Quill
Maguk World
And The Magical Emerald City
In his haversack along with him
He couldn't miss an opportunity
Such as this through the meandering
Babbling riverside
With so many curious visitors this week
It was thoroughly spell binding an enchanted
Adventure
Mr Water Ratty eagerly in response to his mates
Answered chipping in enthusiastically
"What a Wonderful time down the riverside
Serenading with my lovely luncheon basket
Its luncheon rhyme
Now to tell you the secret of the contents
Before we opened it of course

To begin with a serenade

Hambutterbeefmayonnaisetonguefishfillets

Burgerchutneycheesestrawscheesestickscheesecakessalad lettuce

Cabbagemustardceleryparsleypistachiosanchoviesfishfingers

Croissantschickendrumstickssausagerollspoppadums

Piggyinblanketsscotcheggsveggerainbowsandwitches

Quite a mouthful!

Yummmm! Yummy! Slurrrppp......"

He relished with drops of his salivating glands trickling

So much

More than he could practice to serenade

A picnic tongue twister song in just a split second!

Mr Moley and Mr Badger were just

As high in spirits and licking lips

With their little pink tongues

Sipping on their straws on lime cordial, gin and soda water

Lapping up and basking in breath of sunshine air

To relish every little bit in the description

Of his serenading luncheon basket

With gusto they declared

"We'd love to be your guests

Wouldn't we helping ourselves

To every crumb and sandwich

Without saying goes well

With meat and hammage

As goes lugs with luggage"
As they sailed by soon
Bubbles arose from the water
And out popped an otter
Their sweet friend
"Now" remarked he
"Wouldn't I be invited to such
A party picnic as this?
It would be a shame to feed
Gastronomic without passing
Me a fish or mullet
You always would oblige
Without any excuses"
Mr Water Ratty removing two
Big sardines from a tin can
Inside his luncheon basket
And a handful of mullets
Passed it onto the otter
Who happily grabbed it with his snout
And said to the greedy hungry otter
Whilst busily golluping voraciously
"Our dear friend Otter
We would never displease you
Lest you feel we did not invite you
We're off to a peaceful place
Somewhere through the snaky

River bends THAT WAY
Could you please guide us"
The otter happily munching
On the delicious sardines and mullets
Pointed his finger to the left
And described articulately
(For he always loved giving directions
And handy pointers
Forecasting weathers like a weathervane otter)
"Today the creek inlet isles will be sunny
And breezy
As the clouds depart from the mountains
Blowing westward to the isolated green patches
By the sandy beach
It's the best quite place
I've ever experienced on
My travels through the length of this
Riverside, you'd love
The scenery and the colourful
Birds that visit the beautiful
Sprawling branches of the
Swooodennuttie trees
Not to mention the squirrels
And lizards that abound there
Even the windmill house
Can be seen not very far

From its peaceful ambience
You could sport a picture
Near The Old Woman's Shoe by
The hanging willow gardens
If you have carried your camera's
The still landscape is always inviting
For a few cheesy smiles
From good old buddies"
"Thank you"
Replied the Water Ratty
And the three friends
Bid him a goodbye
And continued with sculling their oars
To the left of the riverside
Till they reached the splendiferous
Picnic spot
Bringing boat ashore
And safely placing their oars
To one side of the shaded elm
They got off helping one another
To climb out and into
The beautiful surrounding
Removing their huge picnic basket
And mats
They laid out selecting a spot
Almost close to the riverside itself

And spread one by one the contents
Of the picnic basket
Passing on the ham and bacon sandwiches
And pouring out delicious sweet meads
Salad, hot piping tea and ginger biscuits
That Mr Badger had carried in his thermos flask
And haversack
Whilst he continued to open
Pages from his beautiful illustrated story books
To read further
Whilst tearing a little page for Mr Moley
And handing him his best fountain nib pen
To scribble few lines of poetry
And a wonderful doodle of the rich countryside
The swans that dabbles down the riverside
He made it up himself
Like a lid out of his Lord Byron's head
He evolved one ditty

"THE SWANS......"

"The swans as white as bread
And toasty golden the sunrise
They dabbled with their heads
Dipping into tea the slough
Of the babbling pewter

Whistling away Pheeee pheee pheeeee.....
On the stove like bubbling
Milk and water merry merrily
Now they dabbled once or twice
Inside the river water
And then above to see
Reflections of their graceful
Entourage with necks tails and beaks
They solve the jigsaw puzzle
Of the heart that sleeves
Many men wear
Before they confess true love
To their Juliets
The Romeos dabbled
A Swan Song Entourage
White and peppered
Grey and blue
With sails as one merrily
Oared
Down the babbling brooks
Called Amore
Up and down
And down and up
The swan song ditty
I composed"

At the end of his poetry recitation
Mr Badger, Mr Moley and Mr Water Ratty
All sang together
The famous dabble and travel song
They had learnt in school when they were young
And Mr Water Ratty played along to the beat
Of its Magical melody with snap of fingers
And clapping of hands, music on his bright
Red harmonica!

"MY PADDLE"

"My Paddles green and white
Flushing with silver
Follow the blue bird's flight
Dip Dip and sing
As he dabbles and travels about
So do we now
In our blue and white scull boats
With our glistening oars
Dip dip and sing
Flushing with silver
Follow the swan song tails
And bright blue crested wing
Follow the blue birds flight
Dip dip and sing

Sing sing sing sing sing"

As the valleys and rivers resounded an echo back
With the Ballet High song
Lingering along the windy breath of morning sunshine air
It went like this.......

"A BALLET HIGH"

"Ballet high OOOOOhhh Ooooh Oooooo'
Will call you
Anytime anyday
In your heart you'll hear her whisper
Come away oooohhh oooh ooooo'
Come away
Your own special hopes
Your own haunting dreams
Shimmer in her star ways
And shine in her breeze
In your eyes you'll see her vanish
In the mist
To a distant faraway place
Till she appears dancing once again in your dreams
Ballet high OOOOOOh Oooooh Oooooo
Will call you

Anytime anyday
In your heart you'll hear her whisper
Come away OOOOOOh Oooooh Ooooo'
Come away!"

Whilst Mr Water Ratty had a hand
At fishing sport with his hook, line, fishing rod and tackle
Hooking a worm as his bait
Luckily he caught white baits, minnow
Catfish, Tilapia, anchovies
Even got hold of a King and a Blue Crab
In his little cage
Fighting with its pincers and snapping pliers
Luckily won like a gallant silver shining Knight
Of a fish and sea Rat Battle
He put it inside his net to take home
'Une affaire à convoiter'
'An affair to covet'
A specimen of this special Picnic Tale to remember forever
After their lucky sail boat trip ended
His friends Mr Moley and Mr Badger sufficiently showered
Upon him a round of applause honouring him
With title of "Fisher Ratty of the Century"

Then Mr. Badger pouring more cups
Of his special spice lemon tea

A second serving
To all of his dear friends
And remaining cinnamon buns
Which was a last surprise
To the amicable party of picnickers
Whilst little birds and their friends
The squirrels came by for the
Left over crumbs
Even the lizards got a taste
Of the best Clum May flies
That hovered near their picnic baskets
The wet smudge of chocolate stain on their faces
The ant eaters, ant hogs or ant bears
Along with the friendly rodents
The badger, ratty, moley
Smelt like hot chocolate cocoa fudge
As they burrowed noses and faces inside the grimy mud
Trying to nibble a few earthworms, leeches, slugs
Or ants
Even an extra helping few swarming cluster flies
And jumping lady love bugs and beetles
That surely Mr Toady they imagined
Would love to catch
On such an adventurous picnic as this
By the slick flicks of his long oily tongue
A sport they couldn't deny out beat any time

Anywhere with its interesting time pass munchies
Like a spin of a red dazzling Beetle top
And little flying dragonfly tailed kites
Everyone had a steal of a treasured time and mouth-watering
Ants, worms and insects
And now it was time to pack the huge
Picnic luncheon basket once again
It was easily unpacked
But now packing up
One had to remember the plates
That was around the grass
Hidden spoons and forks
The butter knives and of course
Pepper and salt shakers
And the little mustard pot
Carefully placing all the ingredients
Of the happy luncheon picnic party
Into the luncheon basket
They proceeded folding their mats
And taking a picture only hand drawn
By clever Mr Moley
For they had not brought their camera along
Mr Moley made an exact replica
Of the three cheesy smiles
Imagining him to be there
Standing beside the Old Woman's Shoe

Of the hanging whispering willow boughs gardens
As they circled hands around shoulders
Though he was the centre of attention
The brilliant artist sketching them
SAY CHEESE! And a bunch of red balloons
Then scribbled a rhyme on the post card he painted
As he sang the old nursery rhyme very well

"THE OLD WOMAN WHO LIVED IN A SHOE"

There was an old woman who lived in a shoe
She had so many children; she didn't know what to do
A mole, a badger, a toad and a rat
Contrary to her crocodilian of bats nursery kindergarteners
That hung upside down the roof of the shoe house
Rather tongue tied with shoe laces!
She spelled and teased and raised her cane
And thought them well manners and good ounce of shame
She also gave them a kiss every night if they learnt
How to make butterflies fly from their hats
Sometimes even rabbits, Leonshupony peonies
And derby dragonfly fairies
Like magicians do
From knots, scarves, ribbons, bows and handkerchiefs
Out they flew from nowhere

Till so skilled her little children
Learnt to poke every finger in her crusty pies
Dabbled they witchcraft like experienced crooks
Raised their collars, moles on chins and brows
Along with their meddlesome cats and flying brooms as well
Before she sent them all to bed
In her old little shoe as big as a giant's boot
She gave them some broth without any bread
And whipped them all soundly once more
Then finally she tucked each one to bed
And a kiss on their little foreheads
The old woman who lived in shoe
By the hanging whispering boughs of the willow gardens
They wept whilst all of them slept
Soundly and dreaming in their little beds!"
"The old woman I guess
Must have been a vole or a shrew of a Witch!
Quite a befitting title for old Mother Goose!"
Said Mr Moley to his friends as they
Enjoyed the lovely painting on the postcard
He sketched and with it his beautiful nursery-rhyme!

They wouldn't leave without commenting
About rich Mr Toad missing out all the fun
Who lived right around the extreme opposite
Facing the Dahlia Windmill house on

The picnic site
And how good it would be to have him on
One of their prized picnic boating trips again
Mr Toady missing out the much debated Haggle Pot
Of picnic surprises, red balloons
Love bug Beetles, cluster fly spinning tops
Dragonfly tailed kites and cake slices!
They were planning to visit him
The next day
And made reservations for Mr Badger
To assist along with them
Who they always had to fix a date
Or a special appointment in advance
Mr Badger would be privileged
To accompany them as three
Musketeers on a happy adventure
To riotous Mr Toady's Rich Mansion
Who was always about his wheels in wheels
Maybe sailing one day
Or canoeing then maybe driving recklessly
Through the wild woods, paddling with his
Unicycle or driving his truck
He always had the best from
Clothes to automobiles
Wagons to catamarans, dinghy's and sail boats
He was in fact so blessed

As to come unharmed
As a little fly even after
His many crazy and perilous adventures
As he loved racing through
The wild woods
Once in a while
Or must I say often enough

Before they took turns to settle
Themselves on their scull boats
In charge of the oars and sculls
Mr Moley tried to manoeuvre the boat
All by himself
Though not being experienced
At handling it all by himself
A thorough Greenhorn tipped the boat so badly
That the boat along with sculls fell deep
Into the cold freezing waters along with Mr Moley
Coming to his rescue as swiftly as possible was our hero
Mr Water Ratty with his sleek as shiny velvet coal black
Body dived deep and plumbed the river depths
Swimming bedraggled Mr Moley right
Safely to the top of the surface
Along with the remnants of the soiled huge picnic luncheon basket
And his pair of sculls

Mr Badger quite upset at Mr. Moley
Scolded him very disappointed over the fact
Having lost a scrumptious saving for
'Greedy beggars! Making way for the provender!'
In other words the phrase seemed apt to apply for
Poor Mr Water Ratty's luncheon saved for a rainy day
Loot of Mr Water Ratty's precious hammage
He meant Luncheon Luggage wasted into the cold frozen river
For not having listened to them
However Bonhomie and good humoured Mr Water Ratty
Forgiving Mr Moley's rash decision
To have a hand at the oars all by himself
Condoning all faults and untimely mishaps
Invited all his beautiful compadre's
After their praiseworthy adventure trip ended by the river
For a cup of hot piping Cherokee coffee or delicious hot cocoa
When they finished sailing through a dream like a song
Reenergizing them with some delicious home baked
Butterscotch cookies and sesame doughnuts
Before all seated themselves inside the sail boat
And had a firm grip at the sculls
Once again all settling inside the scull boats
Joined by the three merry rowers
Whilst they sculled their way
Through they spoke, jabbered and tittled-tattled
Right through their enjoyable panorama of journey

Of the latest news in the riverside
The dams and the otter's new shoe
He found maybe a diver's soul
The S.O.S bottles flung out by steam boats
The cloop, clod, clum blue bottles and the leaf miners
Insects and flies hovering
Over picnic baskets
That distracted them like red herrings
From their gossiping
About the egret's lunch of baby fishes
They always stole from poor Mr Otter
Even the Squirrel Natterjacks
Robbing big nuts from Mr March Hares
Tree hole so many fell down there
The Jabbernowlers just
Irritated poor Mr March hare
And they always loved talking about
The recent dam that was a blessed
Gift to all of them
Especially when the weather
Of rains thundered filling it to the brim
They could huddle safely inside their
Holes and burrows
Without a bit of worry over quarry
Digging from it the stone, sand and gray limestone
For making a bridge over troubled waters

Building a bond as solid as the London Bridge
Of friendship famed through generations
So tall and buttering a bridge of sticks, stones
Straw and mud
Of their great wide world
Cheers to a Primitive Life! Hurray!

MR TOADIE
THE OPEN ROAD

Talk about the pot calling
The kettle black
To stir with a ladle
What Mr Toadie often punned
"To hell with the open road
Too much racing I've got to
Zoom Poop Poop Pooopity Poop Poop!
With my horn
O' I wish someone like
Mr Moley, Mr Water Ratty
Or Mr Badger would arrive
Sooner than they promised
To give my animals company
Whilst on my joyride through
The open road
Croak Croak Rippet Rippet!"
The pot calling the kettle black
Was Mr Toadie's bright idea
Racing and landing himself
In unnerving complicated situations
Only his friends could sort out
Avoiding making the call to the police
In most situations

Was he to blame for his rash and reckless
Car racing escapades
As if the open road was not full of
Roadies and car racing nerd nuts like him
Honkering and honking their horns
Their way through the snaky
Lanes of the countryside
If it only hadn't been for
Mr Moley, Mr Badger and
Of course Mr Water Ratty
To having Mr Toady saved in the nick of time once again
Paddling their way
Through their sail boat
Hoping to catch up with Mr Toady
Just in time
Or in a wrinkle of a lagging hour or so
The eeriness of the choppy waves below
And nippy atmosphere above
By the presence of the very enormous
Yellow moon
Looming along the edges of the riverside
And hem of the narrow path
Bifurcating into the woods
Where the large mansion of Mr Toady
Lay sheltered amongst the whispering
Oaks, willows and pines

They placed their oars alongst the shadows
Of the paddock in the barn rack
And welcomed good horse David
Of Mr Toadies Little Caravan Cart
It was so spruce and tidy with everything in place
Just sufficient for the trio
To keep their heads comfortable
In the narrow bunk beds
With a pleasing Canary cage
With two yellow canaries
And a stock of the best scallions, leeks
Potatoes, bag of onions, cilantro, shallots, garlic pods
And red hot peppercorns
In the little kitchen
So that they could pop in
For some hot chicken stew
Or some bubbling coffee brews
To pep them up
Before they delved into the whimsical fads
Of Mad Mr Toadie's ventures
They knew he had taken his
Latest buggy and Broom Broomed away
Out into the open roads
Almost every time landing himself
In a soup as usual
But this time as they decided

To take a pleasurable ride
By the pleasant countryside
Befriending the good sturdy
Little horse David
And tethering upon him reigns
Of the little spruce and natty
Caravan belonging to Mr Toadie
For housing his curious friends
They were in for a rude surprise
Whilst they rambled by their caravan
Into the open road
To their utmost horror they staggered in surprise
And bewilderment
When a ruckus zooming car
A Love Bug jalopy
Came barging right into the peaceful ambience
Lollop, trollop, lopollo, lop!
Gallivanting upon their sweet horse David on a jolly joyride
Almost knocking over the caravan
Luckily into the bushes whilst Poor Mr Toadie
Swerved and crashed into a great big tree trunk
Stunned by his overwhelming experience
Hoping he had no broken bones
Or even his cartilages and carriages spared
From his nasty rash overtaking Beetle Love Bug
Commencing a sad outcome of a joyride of cheap thrills

Sadly would never learn a lesson
To miss out on one of those speedy highs instead of sullen blues
The teaming friends
Mr Ratty, Mr Badger and Mr Moley
Got down the pink and blue
Striped Horse caravan
And quickly assisted Mr Toady
Out from the burning wreckage
Hopefully he was sound and safe
With just a minor cuts and bruises
And complaining as recklessly
As a horn bleep like a Toy Noddy
Whilst the car beetle Love Bug sputtered
Sputter, sputt, sputter, sputtle
Extinguished his jaunty spirits in a crackle and crink
"Tooot Tooootie Pooppity Pooop!
Fresh as a daisical
Am I finished rather
Should I furnish with
A bleep, horn, wiggle or moan"
Not yet finished with the sporty miscalculation override
And then hopping and jumping
Up and down madly as ever
He settled with the car wheel
And horn in both his hands

They had naturally separated from the car
"Am I alive?"
Mr Toad cheerily said to Mr Badger
And Mr Moley
Blaming the pot that stirred the ladle
The pot calling the kettle black
He blamed the interference on the highway
Explaining exasperated and intolerably than it deserved
Blaming his phony actions on account
Because of some stupid herons
Young stoats, weasels and beavers coming across the path
He had to swerve to the right
Almost knocking his good friends
On to the kerb side into the bushes of the open road
As if it wasn't his fault for driving
At such a high abominable speed
I reckon he didn't sense
Danger arising from his usual dare-devil feats
When Mr Moley did complain
To Mr Water Ratty and Mr Badger
"Ahem!.......I guess we should have to do a
Bit of complaining to the police"
Jibing with sarcasm a joke as a warning jolt
At poor Mr Toad, his scarcely credible racing infatuations
And his hopeless wreckage
In efforts to salvage situation
Bring him to his senses and stop his madness

Ashamedly he stopped his friends
Right on their tracks correcting them immaturely
Croaked......
"Rippet Rippet Rippet
It is no sin I say speeding
Poop POOOPITY Booop BOOOPITY!
What is sunshine and adventure meant for?
If they don't go hand in hand
With the Open Road
And my Love Bug Buggy
Instead of just a handful of
Pieces of advice.... But's or If's
But you should
If you didn't
Rippet Rippet!"
They condoning his many faults
And mischievous stunts
Owing to his fanatic love
For riding cars, sail boats,
Wagons or trucks
I mean automobiles of any kind
And types
Water Ratty, Moley and Badger
Settled their grouses with
Their foolish and rich friend
Mr Toady
Amicably and genially

Cautioning him henceforth
To never venture on a whirlwind of
Risk taking sprees
Naturally would land him in a soup
Or a disaster!
Not reacting to his limp excuses
Or shy answers anymore
Made him promise to a sound
Bed rest of thirty days
They even vouchsafed to be his stout Nanny nursemaid
Protectors
And to live with him for a period of thirty engaging days
To provide him an informal kindly gesture of
Serving him breakfast in bed
A quick recovery after his mad mishap
Both sense and sensibility, body, soul and mind
In other words 'Mind over Matter'
'Soul over Sense'
'Body and Meditation'
Or else the matter they pretended
Would be divulged to the police department
In a registrar of complaints
This they decided to do all within their powers
With good intentions
In order to keep Mr Toadie away
From the Open Road

MR BADGER
MRS BADGER

PRIVATE KEEP OUT TOADY'S MANSION AND THE WILD WOODS

"O' how I long for the wild woods!"
Sighed Mr Moley to Badger
And Mr Water Ratty too agreeing
Nodded heads at them
How they missed the beauty and serene life
At their little ground holes
By the Whispering Willows
Though the large mansion
Mr Toady possessed was too splendid for words
It had the slogan

'PRIVATE KEEP OUT TRESPASSERS'

This was done to keep the sly foxes
The enemies of all garden creatures
Surrounding Mr Toady lush mansion
Around the deep wild woods
Mr Toady's rich illustrated mansion displayed all of
His ancient ancestors
Artistic engravings and sketches on huge oil painted
And glossy canvases, porcelain busts

Of his forefathers and hierarchy of jumping toads
Of the lilies and lily pad gardens
Upon the breathtaking pools of long bull rushes
And feathery dandelion puffs
To make wishes come true
For the four friends and their budding friendship
Commencing right from infancy, childhood
To grown up adult age
Priming as blocks of old cheese
Comedians of a replica rodent family
A chip of the old block indeed!

Mr Toady's Dooliyaanah Mansion
As the name suggested dooliyah and daahliyah's
Meaning little darlings and doolings
Charming and quaint faery folk of the Soda Bay inlet
Living around the beckoning waters of the wide wood
Opulence in its narrow islet
He had a sprawling fifteen bedroom mansion
Inherited from his Great Great Great Grand Uncle
Mr Dooliyaanah Little Toad
With turrets, spiral stairways
And spires dating back to the seventeenth century
A newly renovated kitchen and sprawling living room
With a large banquet hall table
For around fifty guests

Great sized balconies and verandas
High ceilings to the very top with classic ancient
Rotating fans, classic bathrooms
And some luxury fittings and bathtubs
Two kennels and a cat house
For his pet Alsatians, Labradors and pussy cats
Nestling right atop the roves
Was an eye-catching crow's nest
To cuddle with a sweetheart
It had parking sheds and garages
For his vast collection of spiffy motor cars
With massive beams and pillars
Supporting the walls of the magnificent mansion
And its splendiferous artefacts
Not to mention his
Great Great Great Grand Uncle Mr Dooliyaanah Little Toads
Grand collection of tobacco smoking chimney pipes
Made of briar wood, meerschaum, corncob, pear-wood
Rose-wood, clay, even some dense grained wood like
Cherry, olive, maple, mesquite, oak and bog wood
Some minerals like catlinite and soapstone
Its pipe bowls decorated by rich carvings and his moulded clay ones
Often with some simple decorations
Some unusual ones like gourds...as in the famous calabash pipe
Pyrolytic graphite its rims covered with a heavy crust of lava

And the bowls a nice thick cake built up on the sides
Both had a strong smell of aromatic tobacco
Whilst smoking his pipe like a gentleman in one ancient
Sketch upon the mansion walls showed he had
Lived a Cretan lifestyle that one viewed from the large balconies
That Cretan soil generously offered olive oil, wheat, wine
Honey, fresh herbs, greens and spices!
"And LOVE!" Mr Water Ratty exhaled
"A bachelor but incurable romantic
Once like a Vampire Popeye Toad sailor man
Who fell in love with a Vampire Olive Oyl Toadess"
Mr Moley commented to Mr Badger making a point
"'ONCE BITTEN TWICE SHY!'
I suppose his poor heart stolen forever! Alas! Fanged!
Drunk to Sorrow! Sorrow laded his blood thirsty spirits!
Dragooned to fall head over heels
Heels over head!
Instead of Knighted and even Gaslighted!
Heartbreak over Romacedom!
He Forfeit his cards
For playing Knave rather fool of hearts
Another Joker Jack trumped all aces over Jill
A poppita for naivess Olive Oyl Toad Papita's clumsy heart"
Mr Badger reminisced as he remembered dear Mr Toady's

Heartfelt sympathies for his rich
Great Great Great Grand Uncle
"Foolishness for toying like a toy toad"
Had sighed Mr Toady to all his friends once long ago
"Heartstrings of my Great Great Great Grand Uncle Dooliyaanah's
Dear fragile and precious heart"
Who Mr Toady had always regarded as a Count Dracula Toad of a
Great Great Great Grand Uncle though reformed of course!
Did herald such news as this from the Toad Hall Books of generations
Passed down in his great grand Library of Toadstools, Vampires and Witchcraft!
Though rich and green like a King Toad Pea
Now rich in poverty like those beatitudes!
Yet his dream to live a simple hermit life
In solace it's beckoning whispers of nature
Turned unhappiness to gladness and woe to happiness
A welcoming Cretan landscape of the surreal Soda water Inlet
The character of the entire location
Was totally faery tale!

Now before the thirty days of promise
To Mr Toady could pass by furtively
Mr Moley however longed to venture all by himself
The next early morning even without a mention

Or a breath to his two friends
A solitary trek to the wild woods
He filled his little haversack with pleasant
Surprises from the pantry
A rasher of ham and two rashers of bacon
A bottle of marmalade and a few toasts
Even a bottle of lemonade
And a few greens, beans and pasta
He rummaged from the huge fridges
Inside the big beautiful kitchen of Mr Toady
Even without his obliging chef Beaver Mr Nuttle
Knowing about his deliberate miscue
That his adventure with rations of home scraps
Would result into a catastrophe
Mr Moley happy and self opinionated
Regarded him being totally self sufficient
In handling such a risky trek as this out by his own
Through the wild wild woods commented
"Certain creatures like mole enjoy finding
Out things by themselves
Whilst other poor creatures like to be spoon fed"
Raising up his collar whilst scampering along
Sang the Jailor song
Of the happy reunion of his three friends
As haply and innocently he ventured out
Rambling into the deep woods beyond

"JAILORS"

How we jailed specimens
Of the hidden holes
Hibernating in winter now spring
Extols
Our treks beyond the hidden vales
Out on our own
Sometimes we oar, sometimes we paddle
Sometimes we ride the song of babble
And the Soda water Inlet Bay
Fills its gurgles and splashes
With our songs and sails
We jailors and jail birds
Begin our stout adventure
Through the thicket like a thief
Through the hills like a rooster
Through the rivers like a lobster
Through the lanes like an eel
We practice our gait till we
Sip with straw, anther and filament
Of the honey pistils of shoe flowers
The Hibiscus and Honey Suckles
And their honeyed vine nectar
That bees often visit us jailors
And jail birds of a sweet sonnet
As sound as the music

DO RE ME FA SO LA TI DOE
And their reverberating echoes
DOE TI LA SO FA ME RE DO
Of the deep woods beyond
The jailors!

And marching up and down the wendans
And curves of the deep deep woods
He began his long arduous journey
He knew he would be home soon
Maybe early evening or so
And catch up with Mr Badger and Mr Water Ratty
For a lovely tea time snack and spice tea
As he rambled through the wide deep woods
He could hear voices of the crows "chak-chak's"
The early morning humming birds, the owls
Hootenanny "Twhu Whit Twhu Whoots" and
Cuckoos "Cu-Coo Cu-Coo"
Croon and hum along
O' wasn't it all so inexhaustible the Jailor song
The intoxicating tillowing and billowing leafy branches of
Sodden and wooden woods
The skies used trees for poetry
Whooshing by the breeze
It sang about the old man wood
Cheery song

"QTEE THE OLD MAN WOOD"

"Qwhooosh, Qwheee, Qpheee, Qteee, Qheee, Qwheee
It's quite mad to use my name Qteak Qwirk or Qtember wood
Is spelled as Quoak or Qobbler Touch Wood!
So Qweeer so weeery rosy!
As cobbler goblins busily makes my lucky shoes to fit each and every
Groove hidden underneath the sud a cutie Qtree roots
My trunk and limbs
As dark as brown tan so queer a leather hide
And torso unusually bark my livery pride
Like a Cobbler Tree House standing aloft it oft' hides
A shiver up spines of busy critters in a fable land
Hopping scurrying soles to climb tap tappity tap up its towering heights
Its soul searching mates and champs
Maybe a squirrel, lizard, dove or sparrow
Even a monkey, bear, frog or a hallow bat upside down to mock and titivate
A serpent to rattle hisses and hypnotise and
bees to buzz and bombilate
Cello and pipe the pied pipers with beaks and talons to match
'We all friends of old man Wood, a chip off the old block of Wood'
Rhyme and rhythms, flight and flibbertigibbets noises
They march and they fight upright and righteously

For a seat under my precious shape and contours
Its long blades and tallow barks
Sat ole man wood under the shade and shadow
Of elm, spruce, adder, birch, pine, willow
His clobbers rare and bright light
Green and sprawling leaves on twigs by far sights revealed
That fell like silent hair and twine so golden and entwined
With fruits, berries and flowers of nig' to nip and nibble
Carving and chiselling
Moulding and meddling
With his branches of nod and nood
Its nodules, stumps and spurs
That crossed and tillowed and stirred
His call of breath and holy wind
That moaned and sighed
Calling all the busy birds to sing
Upon that bough he curtsied so low
A humble old man wood and wind bow and greet sweetly Woodonutie
Hello chipmunks, hallow wood peckers, howdy do Hornbills
Insects one and every kings and kinds
And stood till dusk on his rooted ground
Never to stray from his path
One lonely sodden wooden jungle path
With so many of his old man wood friends
All who encompassed

As they chipped he barked from mighty heavens
On strings and branches so wooden he played wood master
And sang for all the pupputianskins (wood puppets)
Both nigh' through day as lark
As the bird that sings
And blind through the night as black
Where blind bats hang upside down
Hoods off to the ole man wood
Of chips and chops
The wood cutter has come
To bring you down
Like a fire breathing Dragon from Hell's Lair
Alas! Woe Be Me! Please don't I plead! Just hear my song
My prized Blair, orchids and sodden roots on grains of gravel
Let me dip my wooden cobbler toes and polished teak boots into riverbed now
Where frond and fodder, algae and bacteria thrieve
My strange mirrored reflection of pebbles, fungae, weeds, rocks and grass
And the upper sky melts with moaning winds that holler
To paint with poetry, mould like clay breath that fashions
Its wood wheel of pottery and colour our branches that sigh in sorrow
Our flag and anthem on our barks so brown and tan a leather hide
Green as grass and mustard a moss
Said the ole wood man Qtree to the choppy wind

"Qwhooosh, Qwheee, Qpheee, Qteee, Qheee, Qwheee
Qobbler Touch Wood! So Qweeer So weeery Rosy!"

The ravines and the deep stories surrounding them
The fishermen with their nets and tackles and baits
The shepherdess with her solitary repose
And the knights and his amorous valentines
Waiting for him to arrive on his steely horse
In shining armour
As well as the prince kiss the sleeping breathtaking
Beauty of the gales and vales
Bringing her 'Beau Paysage' alive
'La Vue' 'La Nature' like a C'est la vie!
(To accept by sights with resignation her awesome
Splendorous beauty of nature
That cries 'That's Life!' in French)
That hypnotized every living creature
Dabbling in morning treks such as this
Lovely pastime or hobby
Mr Moley indulged in a little nursery rhyme
Song he made up by the crackling voice of
The big black beady ravens for all his friends
Along the way the King and his farm of rye
A hundred miles........

"FOUR AND TWENTY BLACK BIRDS"

Sing a song of sixpence,
A pocket full of rye,
Four and twenty blackbirds
Baked in a pie.
When the pie was opened
The birds began to sing—
Wasn't that a dainty dish
To set before the Mouse king?
The Mouse king was in the counting-house
Counting out his money,
The Mole queen was in the parlor
Eating bread and honey,
The Badger maid was in the garden
Hanging out the clothes.
Along came a blackbird
And snipped off her nose.
Sing a song of sixpence,
A pocket full of rye,
Four and twenty blackbirds
Baked in a pie.
When the pie was opened
The birds began to sing—
Wasn't that a dainty dish
To set before the Mouse king?

They sent for the Rat King's doctor
Who sewed it on again
He sewed it on so neatly
The seam was never seen
That Mr Moley had made up what he heard
Way past pleasant time
Moley had a good laugh
He never amused himself for so long that hard
So many many years till he spruced
Another last cap for the verse
There was such a commotion
That little Jenny wren
Flew down into the garden
And put each their funny noses back again
For y'see black birds
Had stolen all of them
He meant their funny long noses
And short ones too!
All shaped like clothes horses and funny pegs
Just the other day King Water Ratty
Had complained to Queen Moley and Maid Badger
The four and twenty black birds of rye
Began to sing a dainty dish breakfast song
Of Six Pence
Nonetheless bread scrambles egg pie
Scrumptiously prepared for Mr Toad

The offender ravenously hungry
Like those black beady ravens
That often perched talons on the balconies
Of his mansion
To steal and then sing with black hoods and beaks
Their infamous nursery rhyme
Mr Mole had learnt from them of course!

Till it was beginning to get quite a puzzle
The roads seemed to bifurcate into smaller and narrower
Green blotches into nullity and ambiguous
Patches of green labyrinths, bushes and foliage
Strewn in bits and pieces like a jigsaw map
Hewn over the thick gross undergrowth here and there
That Mr Moley could no longer recognise at all
Even if he had a map which by any chance
he'd forgotten to carry
Now he sat on a stump of wooden trunk
He was lost and grimaced to himself
"What a miscue of an adventure
I've landed myself in a soup
O' Ratty where are you?
O' Badger I hope I see your little ground hole soon
Who would possibly help me now
I guess it's even beginning to turn dusk
If only I'd let my friends know

Of my foolish trek beyond the wild wild woods"
And for long he sat on the stump
Till he noticed the ground holes smile
As if unevenly and zig-zaggedly
With fangs like Draculas
And sharp evil eyes gleaming through them
Soon darkening skies
That almost fell like a heavy cloud
Upon this strange valley
So many ground holes and so many
Sinister devious weevil eyes
"Whoever could they be?"
Moaned Mr Moley to himself
Quite exasperated by the turn tale of doosy events
So quickly and suddenly
As the drape of the large blue moon
Surrounded the acres of the dwindling copse
Like Hoes and Dao's of Lord Tao's spectre
Sights disappearing before his very own
Steely pair of pale blue grey eyes
He saw the large Alice Rabbit hopping
Wildly and running
As if he were saying to himself and Mr Moley
"Skiddaddle Skiddy
Run for your lives
The skillet creatures of the Underwood holes

Will fry you like a noodle in a bowl
Of crisp insects"
"Whatever could he mean by that?"
Thought Poor Mr Moley
And soon taking the good advice
Of the madly hopping bugs bunny
He followed him in the direction he
Hopped wildly to another strange hidden
Destination where poor Mr Moley popping himself inside one
Deserted hole soon reached to a conclusion
The dark eerie night had landed many
Unusual critters hiding inside abandoned holes
Of the Underwood world
And comforted himself thinking
"Those scary eyes must have been
Just a clan of friendly furry gerbils
Or noisy Mole Rodents like me!
Maybe a good knot of fiery vampire toads
Camped inside for safety
Or just maybe"
He gave a shadow of a doubt
Some unsettling worry
"A camp of upside down wolf faced bats
With shiny whiskers of gloss"
He shivered right to his tingling spine and remarked
"Pythons or poisonous cobras or the venomous great mamba"

Then maybe comforting himself again
"A horde of hamsters like roulette
They played a deck of card games
In underground holes and cavities
Or herd of unusual guinea pigs
On this day grinning evilly
Hats off to their scary hoods....
Their strange discourse of grunts howls
Growls, shudders, creaks, hoots, howls, roars
Grumbles, groans and moans
Scary confabulation in Chinese Whispers
(Distorted messages being passed around in whispers
A game often played by naughty elves and faery folk critters)
A mystery likes Chinese Chequers
With a star of a Chinese Flag
Or on chess board with sixty four squares
Its chess (draught) pieces- Queenside and Kingside
Amidst a Great Wall of China"
The barricade fortress of the imperial stony Weir
Built across the streams of riverside
And the mammoth wind fan propellers
of the dusty Windmill Farm
That loomed somewhere nearby the bracketed picket fences
Further beyond the wild wooden thicket
He could see clearly rotating its pixels
Generating current and electricity

Like heads of a Wind Turbine Windmill Dahlia
"But a skulk of sly foxes....."
Those he had to be careful about
At least till morning crept back
And the sun shone gloriously again
Would he be able to make it home
To Mr Toadies Mansion
Till then he hoped some one
Would answer his prayers
Maybe his loving friends
Mr Water Ratty and Mr Badger

In the evening on the other end
At Mr Toady's house
Mr Water Ratty emerged from one of
The rooms where he was beginning to get bored
Looking after Mr Toad and chit chatting
With him about all the rest of the days
When they would help him clean
All his invaluable racing cars and motor bikes
Boats, trucks and Daggone! Wagons
But now he wished to speak to Mr Moley and Mr Badger
Mr Badger however was busy reading
His fairy tale novels
And didn't mind the company of himself
So Mr Water Ratty started to call out

"Moley Moley where are you
Dear Old Buddy?
Do come out
We'd have a cup of warm basil and tomato soup
Stirred up by the chef Beaver Mr Nuttle
And a good helping of tomato beans
With cheddar cheese and crusty fig pie"
Alas! There was not a sound or whimper
Even a breath of his dear friend Mr Mole
Then the chef Beaver Mr Nuttle
Informed worried Mr Water Ratty that Mr Moley
Had packed a ration of food scraps into his haversack
And told him not to tell anyone
That he was gone out
And would be soon back by sunset for tea
Mr Water Ratty sensed danger
He should have been home by now
Then girding around his waist a belt
And a gun into its holster
He carried with him a stout cudgel
His hat from the peg
And his shiny galoshes
He set out into the terror of the wide wood side
To search for his dear friend Mr Moley
With the kindly assistance of Mr Badger
Donning his overcoat

Cane and his large gumboots
Cinching their belts around waists
And their stout cudgels by a hook

MRS
BADGER

DULCE DUMON 'HOME SWEET HOME'

Crunching and crackling through the
Fallen leaves dry and withered away
Like a heap of rubble or a nest of Drone Bumble Bees
As if 'twas autumn or fall
With their rubber gumboots and galoshes
Through the tillowed fields
And the ploughed furrows
They at last arrived at the woody jungle
Where they guessed their dear friend Mr Moley
Had lost his way
With torchlight's they entered through the living
Bracken and thick green foliage
In the bitter dark night
As if it breathed in and out like a green dragon
Puffs of cold shivery breeze
Through its sharp and tangy air
Its sodden musty mouth of the wooded cavity
Released
They had to find in time
Before he was caught, GOD FORBIDS! Eaten or even fell
In some strange deep ravine or into a hidden pit
All thoughts raced their poor minds
Badger and Water Ratty
Astutely beholding their torch lights over heads

Through the shrubs and wavering grasses
Started calling out
"Mr Moley Moley
Come out wherever you are
It's us your dear buddies
You'll be in safe hands soon
Don't worry
Mr Moley Mr Moley"
Soon they heard a whimper
Right through one cotton picking grey colossal
Cloud so dark almost falling inside a deep path
That bifurcated from the edge of the fork
That Mr Moley had long before time ran into
From those evil moving menacing blood thirsty
Blood curdling Eyes
But with the glare of their bright torchlight's
They felt safe and plucking their gimp
Traced the sound of silent whimpers
As if a cry for help emitting
From inside the thicket of the strange
Forked wooded lane
There was Mr Moley sitting duck
In one little underground hole
They could make out his warm toasty beanie
He'd worn that had chequers
Just like the mystery of Chinese Chequers

They played so often
Only now amplified the murmurs
Along the Whispering breeze
Chanter and chunners
And groans and mumbles
Of the Faery Beasts and Faeries
Inside the wooded way
As well the runny Fawcett of the rippling waters
Of the riverside along the Soda Inlet Bay
They giving him a hand brought him up
To the surface and dusted
All the dried mud, leaves and sprockets
That he used to camouflage his hiding
Even the chameleon hiding inside
The hole almost the colour of
Brown and green
Got surprised by the twosome
Adventurous jesty saviours come to save
Dear Old Mr Moley
Moley ecstatic over his timely rescue
Wailed joyously hugging his friends dearly
"A friend in need is a friend indeed!
My dear comrades Badger and Water Ratty
Oh! How miserable was I but now
Am filled with unending happiness just seeing your faces
Makes me feel how lucky I am to be saved

From my nightmarish dream in the wild woods
I dread played a game so foul
As a horrid encounter of ghosts
And hidden holes filled with those devious sly eyes"
Mr Badger patting his shoulders
And making him feel at home once more
Without beating around the bush
Said to him
"Dulce Dumom
Home Sweet Home
Please come along Mr Moley
With me to my little underground hole of a tunnel
It isn't very far from here
You shall soon meet my wife Mrs Badger
All who are in trouble get solace over here Indeed!
My place is warm, cosy, spruce and comfortable
Every once a while do creatures
Stir up my doorbell
And I give them a handy escort
Maybe those who lost their way
Or wishing for help to find
The correct address
Winter after winter
Through sloe and frost
Chilblains, nips, stings and frostbites
Rain, autumn, fall or summer

Maybe because of roughity of weather
Or in due course abandonment by cruel fate
Come to my hearty hole
Welcomed by my hardworking wifey Mrs Badger
You will be thrilled to be acquainted
With her lovely warm apple pies
Savoury Chicken strudels, homely beef stews
With noodles and American elbow macaroni Goulash
She is a darling
And wouldn't least mind a bit
Wayfarers especially my true friends
To her splendid care"
"Truly", Mr Water Ratty commented in great awe
As he was used to the outdoors
So often sauntering through the wild woods
And had met Mrs Badger once or twice
But never forgot her kind Queenly hospitability
Soon as they started walking
The rustling wind moaned through the trees
The aoelian sound it made by the moaning
Blowing and hustling through the leaves and
Branches sounded as if it played hauntingly music
A violin with a bow
Harp with fingers
Or piano with soul
Their little hearts beat aloud like drums

As they waited to be safe in Mr Badgers cosy Dulce Dumom
Little deep hole home haven.........Sweetly at home!
As they crunched through dried leaves and debris
Green ferns and grasses
With their leathery moccasins
Rubber galoshes and gumboots
Making their way tother side
Of Whispering Willows
To a little underground hole
Where the address nameplate
A bright bulb flickering over it
Read
"Mr and Mrs Badger
The way for lost souls
And to Heaven"

"What a good sign post"
Sighed Mr Moley
However just before they could
Step inside the natty and spruce little bottom
Hole into the deep roots of his property
Mr Moley had a bad blind fall over one of
The thick roots of the Banyan Tree
A big cut covered his knee
And thick red blood droplets dripped from the open wound
Mr Water Ratty and Mr Badger

Helping him on his feet
Wiped away the streaming tears
With their handkerchiefs
Tied one around his leg
And helped him climb through
The underground hole
Of Mr Badger's sweet repose
"Dulce Dumom
Home Sweet Home"

Mrs Badger was plump and fat
As plump as a little brown and black goblin
With a black beauty spot right above her snout
And silvery white whiskers
So she looked old as if she had aged with wisdom
Of a wise old witch
She invited her Dear husband Mr Badger and all his friends
Giving a warm hug to shaken up Mr Moley
Making him comfortable on the easy chair
As if she was an infirmary nurse
Seeing poor Mr Moley cry inconsolably
In utter desperation over his blind fall
She assisted with some First Aid Kit
Cotton, bandages and Dettol disinfectant
To cover the glaring gash with a Band-Aid
Soon donning her bright orange apron

Retired into the well manicured kitchen
To cook for her guests
Whilst they adventured into the house
Introspecting its many long tunnels
That divided into spacious chambers
Down the deep earth
So muddy, acrid and musty!
They saw how hot, hollow and airless it was inside
Though they were quiet used to it
And yet how spotless and clean
After they settled down on the massive
Slabs of dining chairs
The Dinner bell lady none other than
Mrs Badger Mistress of the house
Rattled and belled a funny Mouse bell
Chiming in a little faery note couplet
Of the Golden Dinner Bell Faery

"THE GOLDEN DINNER BELL FAERY"

Hood, needles and nud
Good Wood Bud Bood Lood
Lud Loon Sud Sun and Sood
Stood the Dinner Bell Golden Faery
In the forest Dell's heart
To ring her bells of glory
Golden and Gorge
River and Lodge
The banquet lay on the table of grass
Where elves, bunnies, pixies, goblins, gnomes and faeries
Drank from the glass goblets of sheer as crystal riverbanks
So clear
That flowed without a flaw
Through the unending gorge and valleys
Rivers, mountains and lodges
Of the soothing landscape of Maries golds
Sunflowers, Buttercups, Hyacinths, Dahlias, Violet shies
Primroses, Daisies, Hibiscus and Daffodils
Perfumed and sweet smelling like vanilla pods
Strawberries Blueberries and Butterscotch ice creams
And cones of Raspberries
Anthem lanes of Chrysanthemums
Madonna Lilies, Lantana Lollies and Peonies Leonshuponies
Derby Dragon flies of the great rivers and valleys

Stooges and Dwarves
Of Snow White's Beautiful glass coffin
Of eternal beauty where she slept so peacefully
Stood so white on the blanket of Snow
The Porcelain Dinner Bell Faery
Painted like gold and shining
Starry and dewy
Her bones of china with first dew drops of Sunshine
She rang her bell loud and clear
That echoed through the mountain tops, cliffs and valleys
She rang her bell to last
Through her forest story
The smell of toasting, burning and roasting
A stove on the firewood
The sound of crackling, crunching, munching and rustling
By leaves on their wooden barks
Of the hollow faery woods
Where faeries leer through its secret nooks
Jumping, hopping, leaping, skipping
Tossed, swam and crawled
To glorify and glory
The sun, sud and stony
The leaves, wood and bony
Like ebony and ivory statues
All made of gold golden and glowing
And the porcelain golden

Faery of the woods
The Dinner Bell Little Lady
Soon sang her anthem prayer
To the Lord
Before everyone finished licking their plates
With tongues, teeth, beaks, snouts, mouths, spoons and forks
Bowing lowly
Mumbling slowly
Chewing and relishing to their last morsels and bits
Of savoury glands watering and
Delectable palates full of taste
With palettes paintbrushes and colour with nature they paint
She blessed the food they ate
The Grace Before Meals
Bless us O' Lord
Of the valley, mountains and fields
Of the church mice, badgers, toads
Mole hills and bunny holes and field mice burrows
Scurrying feet like pitter-patter of raindrops
And these thy precious gifts
Which we are about to receive
From thy bounty
Through Christ our Lord Amen
Before we begin our Pilgrim Journey
Through Whispering Willow Woods
Hood, needles and nud

Good Wood Bud Bood Lood
Lud Loon Sud Sun and Sood
Stood the Dinner Bell Golden Faery
In the forest Dell's heart
To ring her bells of glory
Golden and Gorge
River and Lodge

Mrs Badger went on to explain.....
"Still the story of the Bell Lady
Was not over yet
One day the Porcelain Dinner Bell Faery
So golden and strong
Her China glass broke to smithereens Alas!
No bell could be heard
No music could be stirred
In the magic woods deep yonder
Even the birds and the buzzing bees
The animal's, goblins and the pixies
Tried to gather for dinner
But had lost spell of the time
That the bell faery did remind
And now all creatures sullen, crestfallen, glum and morose
Waited for the blanket of snow
To cover the hazy hills
And sturdy mountains

The green orchards
And grassy glens
The flowers were hidden
Now by the carpet of fresh fallen snowflakes
The silver moon shone in the grey sky
Full of moonlight
And the stars as if they melted
With huge glistening tears
Looked like tear drop icicles of the starlight faeries
Yonder the black night
However soon came a Santa Sleigh
With his reindeers so many and gay
They leapt and bound and reached
The ground where the smithereens
Of the bell faery lay
Soon rhymed a spell Dear Santa
And said to all the bits and pieces
Of the China Clay
"Wake up! Wake up! Dear!
Its dinner time and time to ring
The bell under the skirt
You once played
The music that called
All to the table of grass
And the clear riverbanks
With crystal water drops

In shiny glass goblets as sheer
A toast to cheer! Luck and more Lady Luck!
She arose and the bits and pieces
Were joined back together
Into a new Bell Doll
Faery of the Midnight Lantern
Here she stands
In the silent night
Ringing her bell Ding Dong Ding Dong!
Like a Faery Tinkerbelle
Ding! The King has come
Dong! We adore the faery who sings his praises aloft
Ding A Ling A Ling A Ling! We traverse so far
To hear Ding Dong! Her Tinkerbelle Song
A Ling! With her lovely mandolin and harp
Ding! Taverns light house and towers
Dong! Are you sleeping Brother John and Sister May
Ding Dong Ding Bells Ding A Ling!
Ding! Here comes December and the time to feast at last
A Ling! To call creatures Mother Nature
To her dinner table once again
The table of grass
Along riverbanks clear as crystal or shiny glass goblets as sheer
Now lit with candlelight and her rich transparent porcelains
The story of the Dinner Bell Faery
Of gold and light

Ding A Ling A Ling Ding Dong!
Her bells jubilantly extolled
Of humanity, its faery tale creatures and humankind"

All clapped and marvelled at her beautiful
Poetry
Taking a bow before her audience
She rang the Dinner Bell Mouse again
And invited two brothers
Hedgehog little and hedgehog great
A well-mannered stoat and
A kindly old weasel
All of them so to say lost wayfarers
Of the deep woods
Who strangely found help and were welcomed
By kind Mr Badger and Mrs Badger
Into their warm and cosy hearth
A safe haven for all lost and weary!
Each explained with thorough deliberation
Perplexities and oddities
They faced above the sometimes cruel
Upper world of the woodland and their
Jinxed rules for survival of fittest

After an exchange of tit bits and
Good gossiping Mrs Badger

Came up with some half boiled eggs in eggcups
Cheese omelettes in her frying skillet
Warm beef stew soon followed in a big corrie cauldron
Along with toasted bread and bakers Brun Pao
She then brought out porcelain plates
With separate large bowls, silver spoons
Silver forks, a sharp knife to cut the Brun Pao's
And a serving ladle for the stew
All fitted inside her large apron pockets
Which she neatly arranged on the long dining table
And served delicious meal into the bowls and plates
For everybody
Not forgetting her salt and pepper shakers
And her little mustard pot
A must with any dish she believed
Like a sprinkle of paprika, Tobasco and onions along with it
A wit of wisdom, tongue and cheek
She would often cherish her husband's guests
As her own family and friends
A tasty bite for the hungry and a mug of warm saffron milk
For the thirsty voyagers
Far away from Mr Toady's rich mansion
To the wooded Primitive Life once again!

Though it soon turned frosty
As the temperature within had

Turned freezing
I guess snow had covered
The deep woods with its
Sugar coated blanket
As humbug Frosty the snowman
Encircled his shuddery breath around the nippy air
Making funny patterns of icicle shapes
Around the upper opening of the
Hidden hole
No more would Mrs Badger
Have to worry about using her broomstick
To brush the fallen leaves of boughs
Dead leaves and branches
From the door post of her comfortable Hole end
Now Mr Ratty, Mr Moley
Along with Mr Badger and the rest
Would have to help shovel snow off the entrance
So that anybody in dire need of assistance
Could read the door post and 'brinnng' the door bell
Promptly to avoid any turbulence and further upheavals
Of the gross weather above their cosy hearth
The next joyous day early in the morning
A whiff of baked strawberry cake
Wafted through the chilly air and Mrs Badger
Offered nice and big wedges
After which a bowl of cereal and oats followed

With a cup of hot piping cocoa milk to rest jaunty guests
Of the strange and happy badger household

"I think I have lost my way
To my precious home"
Cried Mr Moley to Mr Badger and Mr Water Ratty
Reminiscing fondly about his dear house
In a deep hole he missed so much
Sighed sorrowfully again and again
With deep furrows on his forehead
Every time he explained so very unhappily
"O' I am so lost
O' so very lost
I want to see my home again
The sweet home sweet breath so unforgettable
And the smell of fresh paint, my foiled attempts
At spring cleaning and white washing
That still has to be finished
All because we decided to rat and roll
The dice over to Mr Toady's hall
And now my little home has disappeared
O' I am so lost
O' so very lost!"
After he had finished wallowing in
Self pity for quite some time
"Poor Mr Moley" Mr Water Ratty and Mr Badger sighed

And contemplated how they would help him reach
The Mole End of his happy story
Mr Badger said to his dear friend
"Don't worry dear old chum
We shall help you find the exact spot
Now would we all not want
To taste some delicious home baked muffins
You always talked about
You loved baking them on cold
And snowy days like this"
After which Mr Water Ratty continued to say
"Now now we shouldn't debate much
As it is we already have forgotten
About Mr Toady
And I wonder what he is up to now
After we promised to keep him company
Till he could keep off his crazy passion
Irresistible rat racing Toad desires
Of race driving through the open roads
I guess he hasn't changed a bit
But now I guess Mr Moley
Is getting a bit depressed
Far away from his cosy Mole End
I guess we should first and foremost definitely
Begin the day
Helping him to finally cap

Dolce Dumon

Home Sweet Home

By camping finally the last straw

At his mole end

That is as soon as we can find it"

That roused in all the three friends

As well as poor sad Old Mole

A burning spirit of adventurous riot

Once more

To find his begging hole of a home destination

Then Mr Badger biding his wife a tearful farewell

Mrs Badger along with the well mannered stoat

Kindly old weasel and Hedgehog junior and senior

Started waving "Goodbye Goodbye" "Goodbye"

Back at them in their squeaky soft voices

Soon Mr Water Ratty, Mr Moley and Mr Badger

Most joyously began

Climbing up the hidden tunnel up Badger hole

To uppity uppity the earth's crust

Where at the topmost turret of the door hatch above

Was Good old otter standing near the door opening of the entrance

Peeking to see if all was well with his friends

Just a next-door friendly neighbour door to door visit

Their hole to hole end!

He often loved doing so and hoped to be of help

To anyone in trouble
Unwaveringly waiting to be of assistance
He had learnt from the faery folk critters
Of the Whispering Willows
About the strange case
Of Mr Moley's disappearance
And by strange coincidence
Or by telepathy knew of his whereabouts
Right down in Mr Badgers hole-end
Whatever you may call it, maybe E.S.P
Extra sensory perception Indeed!
Therefore had come to enquire
From the others what really had happened
But now seeing the happy expressions
And countenances that showed
Satisfaction after a hearty breakfast and
Enjoyable dinner the previous night before
Smiled at his friends
And asked them curiously
"Where are you off to my dears?
Would you want me to aid you
With any useful pointers, tips or directions?"
As if he knew through E.S.P
What they really wished
And that was home of dear Mr Mole's End
Mr Moley crying out into sobs of frustration retorted

To the helpful Mr Otter
"I know the odd ends of rat holes
And burrows of rabbit holes
But where O' Dear has my
Little Mole End disappeared
Would you ever know the way?"
Not to say Mrs Badger had made them wear
Her best hand knitted sweaters
She was an experienced
Knitter of sweaters and cardigans
And had made thirty three of them
Kept in her little closet deep in the burrow hole
Which she distributed to each
Before they commenced on their next journey
To find Mr Moles house
So nice and warm covered in the
Best Mohair knitted fur
They continued to explore
Into the wild woods thither with the directions
That Mr Otter provided them
Further he proudly explained to them
"I know in and out the lanes
Through this forest
Even if I were blindfolded"
Then with lively animation on his face
A slick black oily coat full whiskers and facial expressions

He described the famous en route that
Mr Moley often took to his little mole-end
Which was through the sheep farms
And the sheep pen in the rustic countryside
That unravelled further end of the deep woods
They guided by Otters precise
Fingers, flippers and tails
Decided to walk through the rustic countryside
By the rivers along the church steeple belfry
It was Christmas once again
They decided they must reach Mr Moley's
House early by noon
To taste his Christmas Muffins
He had baked and left on the trays
With a lot of unfinished spring cleaning business to do
Mr Moley was desperately waiting to reach
His far sided place of his cosy Mole End
As he clutched to Mr Badger's walking cane
To support the leg he had injured
Soon after a good distance through the woods
They smelt the varnish of paint
Unmistakably it was none other
Than Mr Moley's Holey
His Home sweet Home
Its unforgettable breath
And everything he babbled about like a baby

Was left just like he described on the deep end of the hole
The paintbrushes, paints, the cookie tray with cookies
And even the oven door left open
The muffins arranged on the little table
With lovely Poinsettias made of crepe paper
For Mr Moley was a skilled artist
In making bouquets of flowers
He settled on his cushiony sofa
With one jute mattress underneath it
Nothing much in his bare room
Only a cupboard
Quickly freshening up and lighting up
The furnace to keep them warm
Mr Water Ratty helped to put the fire wood
They had collected on their way
Whilst Mr Badger helped himself to
Those lovely fudge brownies
And the oven baked muffins
Were put to heat up again
350 degrees fahrenhiet
Till the smell wafted gingerly
Above Mr Moley's little hole into the freezing atmosphere
Full of deliciously toasted smoke of muffins
That they nibbled into
Filled with raisins, cashews and nuts
Those little neighbourhood squirrels had gifted Mr Moley

From their caskets
In exchange for his tasty muffins when they were ready
Mr Moley was a kind and generous soul
And always gave his friends his mothers delicious
Recipes and they obliged him with
Maybe a few precious ingredients
Flour, sugar, eggs, raisins and nuts
With friends as these he was never short
Of anything at all
And cuddled with a cosy warm blanket
As Mr Water Ratty prepared them
A warm cup of hot coffee
Over a choir singing carols
Its lingering music carried by the wind and breeze
Blowing above the mole end hole
The Master Gerbil
And a bunch of field church mice
Singing at the end of the miry
With their bright lit lanterns
Mufflers, woolly cardigans and warm mittens
Christmas Yuletide song
The First Noel

"THE FIRST NOEL"

The angels on their harps
And the shepherds on the fields
All looked above the shiny star
That travelled way afar
The three Kings of the East
Caspar, Melchior, and Balthasar
Wise men of the 'Star of Magi' in Bethlehem
Then Mary, Joseph
Looked at the sky
With angels singing lowly by
The cradle of the hay stable
Underneath the head of the Lord
He was rolled in a simple cloth
Right from his head to his chin
Even his body and legs
They were bare
Only wound delicately in linen
He raised his hands
From his swaddled cloth
And Said the Master Lord Baby
To all who loved the King
The First Noel
And the Star
Shall guide you through eternity

When Master and his people
No longer slaves to darkness and evil
Obey and watch
The bright Christmas Star
Sail merrily in the sky
Like a bauble of a Christmas Tree
Beyond the blue rivers so serene
A solace for all seeking
Love, Peace and Joy
The First Noel
The Angels did sing

So the trio climbed up the
Mole's End to hear them sing
They even heard the chink
In their little bowls
As the passersby
Dropped a few cents
For the busy carol singers
The choir singers were creatures
Like porcupines, stoats, rats
Gerbillies and weasels
The other faery critters church meeces
Who had who joined in
Coming out of the nearby church were
Waiting to be generous in the

Spirit of Christmas day
Just to prove to the world
Pen against sword
Brains against brute
And love against hatred
The true Christian faith rekindled
With church mice and gerbil masters
Of the church

COURT

MR TOADY IN A SOUP

Making good his escape through the open window of his room
Mr Toadie set out straight his mind to make good
Another careless windblown
Trip to the open inviting wooded lanes of wild woods again
After his friends had tried hard to keep him locked
Behind doors inside his mansion room
As much could be described about Mr Toadies
Gregarious and pompous personality
Loving to host lavish balls, dinner and tea parties
Inviting several of his many famous upper crust society
Barons, baronesses, counts and countesses
Stoats, weasels, ferrets, beavers, hares and distinguished meeces
Not to mention Mr Toad was more or less a clotheshorse
He selected from his vast closet room
His brand new ruby red goggles
And matching cap, gaiters
An enormous overcoat, breeches and red boots
Then straddling like a war horse
To paint the town red
Swaggering down the steps like a Royal Toad King Maharajah
Before he mounted inside his brand new buggy
Classic Chevrolet Impala motor car
Drawing on his gauntleted gloves
He was set to race the open road by the moors and fields

Once again
Just in time arrived the trio Mr Badger, Mr Moley
And Mr Water Ratty to much alarm of the high spirited
Creature now looking aghast like something the cat dragged in
Agitated, limp and sore over the fact
His actions of defiance would be dealt with severity
Upon seeing strong unbending resolution on his friends faces
To stop him dead in his tracks
Before he could complete his half baked mission
Annoyed by the interference of his three buddy mates
He quickened the pace of his steps
Towards the red Chevrolet Impala buggy
Hoping to race away
An intense impulse one Frenzied Feverish Fervor
To race wild wooded Froods, Franes, Frivers and Fralleys
In les bois of French alphabet F 'Fun in Jest'
Meaning woods, lanes, rivers and valleys on a
Frightful Frace (Fray Fracas and Ruckus race jalopy)
Funny bag of nerves, jitters and reflexes
However Mr Badger got into his car before Mr Toady tried
Racing off and breaking all rules
Mr Badger caught hold of the steer wheel and
Swerved the car right into the garage
And locked the doors with the help
Of the house maid
Shut away the garage and hid the keys

Somewhere safe in a secret vault
Where Mr Toady could never find
Then turning towards Toady
The three friends confronted him
Challenging him to stop this nonsensical business
At once
Or else he would be locked behind his bedroom doors
Explaining him the seriousness of the matters
That landed him in the same jigmaroles or rigmaroles
He so often sadly faced......Strident toned Police officers
Cloyingly tasting medicines and grim nurse maids
Even knocking over somebody in his rash adventures
They had to take these stringent measures
And lock him up in a high room
To guarantee his safety measures
Like a goofy Prince or a Princess Rapunzel up a tall fortress
As soon as the door was locked
Peeping through the keyhole
He began defending himself
Hoping somebody would hear his lamentations
"I only wanted to BROOM BROOM! Away
On my Red Chevrolet Impala
Away into the furling mists of the wayward
Countryside
Among the mystery vales and hidden dales
Be a sport someone open the doors

Please let me out

BROOM VROOM BROOM!
BO BOP BLOOP BIBOP BOPOPITTY BOP BOO HOO!
BOO HOO!"

As if after advising the impertinent fool

Who looked almost as if he would listen to them

Even after repeatedly persuading him to stop

His bohemian lifestyle

And squandering away the wealth of

His Great Great Great Grand Uncle Mr Dooliyaanah Little Toad

On his trendy expensive tastes

Clothes horse obsession and car driving fads

Gallivanting rascally on his absurd car racing ambitions

Spiralling into ignominy and curses of his fellow creatures

Toadie not paying heed to any reason

Continued on and on ranting and raving

Inside the four corners of his large mansion room

About his missed opportunity to rat race

With his classic red Hound Bound Chevrolet

Impala Motor-car

His cries went on deaf ears

And since the door remained shut

Behaving skittishly like a cat on hot bricks

Who couldn't be pinned down

He started to pantomime the car steer wheel

Breaks, accelerator and clutch
His obvious fantasy to hi-jack or car jack and zoom away
Into oblivion
He would remain there locked up the tall tower room
Decided his wise friends till he came to his senses
Each one of his friends made arrangements
To bring him food and refreshments
Everyday into his secret chamber
Till his revolts, insults and abhorrence's
Would come to a gradual halt
Then Mr Toady over two days of strict vigilance
Took to promising them
He'd never take the car out
On his road rage excursions
But rather they help him
To sort out varnish, paint
And repair the anchor hooks
And helms of his sail boat contraptions
This they agreed and arrived at a truce
Terms of the condition that
They put forth to stubborn Mr Toady
That hence he would not dabble
In anything that rolled on wheels
Even for that matter a bicycle
Or unicycle
For now it would only be oars and sails

Surf and turf the tides brought in
Of the Soda Inlet Bay
Like his teaming guardian angels
They watched day by day
His every move and breath
Till one day Mr Toady decided
He was tired of fishing and sailing
And wished to move into town
Walking and strolling naturally
This they allowed without his wheels
Not knowing the soup Mr Toad would
Land himself in
As soon as Mr Toad reached
The Blue Whale Inn
He resolved to listen to his old buddies like a saint
Without a masque of paint!
Staunchly and stoically abiding by
The promise he made to them
But just outside was a temptation
He could hardly resist
A Brand New Red Dashing
Brute of a flashy red Lamborghini
With its doors wide open
Even without an owner attending to it
Thoughts raced through his pensive mind
"At last my dream comes true

Hijack a car and car snatch a ride
Racing it top speed BROOM VROOM!
Through the pleasant countryside
Bodkins and Limekins!
Let's pull my gaiters up
Breeches above my knees and my
Cloak to my collar
I'm not wasting a minute"
And BROOM VROOM
The zooming car sped
So fast till it reached the maximum speed limits
And soon beside the honking car
Arrived a Police Man on his motor bike
Telling Mad Mr Toady to stop the car heist
Shouting at the top of his lungs
"Hey Mister
Stop I say at once
You'll be fined for sure for such
Bad behaviour"
Mr Toady with the rush of adrenaline
Bursting into spurts of green blood
Through his blue blooded veins
Throbbing as fat slugs on his forehead
He was stopping for no fool
And went racing ahead speeding intolerantly
Explaining like a goonk gobbledegnook of a crook

"Never not now and not ever
Even for a well behaved officer hoodlum Mister Stoat"
Speeding another fast couple of kilometres
As fast his gauntlets could race
The steer wheel which was kept
Away from him hidden for so many many days
Almost a year now
He raced through the valleys and
Lanes, woods past rivers and mountains
Down creeks and fountains
In a Hex v/s Rex (evil spells v/s unforeseen law suits
That it would ultimately result in)
The car going absurdly haywire in circles
And at last without even a hopeless bit
Of remorse over his foolish actions
A hoist by one's own petard!
The whole squad force of police Stoats were
Behind poor Mr Toady
At last his car I reckon stopped
By the tracks of the chugging steam engine
Smoke and dust escaping through the bubbling hot cars engine
Hot as smouldering red hot picket wires
And soon he got off to be handcuffed
In chains by the terrible police officer
Mister Stoat and Hound Baskerville Sergeant of Police
Despite of the many efforts of his good friends

To keep him out the court and prison
Now he was summoned the very next day
And today it was inside a cell
Where he had to sleep the night
Till his friends would appear at court
For the hearing by the Owl of a judge
Who would read out the final decision and full verdict
Over such an unruly behaviour
Terror of the Highway!
His fine panoply soon evaporated
With a cross sullen expression on his
Sagging face
Each muscle loosely hung in exasperation
Over the sentence to be rolled out
By the Owlet judges and Stork, Pelicans, Herons
Quails and Flamingos-Members of the trusted jury
He giggled feebly from one to another
Appealingly
Seeming quite to understand the seriousness
Of the matter
The judge after hearing the jury
And the convict
Came to a conclusion
Whilst his faithful buddies rapt with
Whatever decision would be announced
'Come What May'

Or regrettable consequences of his foolhardy choices
Felt sorry for their dear chum Mr Toad
The judge declared
Pounding his hammer of justice and
Measuring salts in his weighing scales of injustice for poor Mr Toadie
"Twhu-Whit-Twhu-Whoots
To whosoever it may concern
This is concerning Mr Toad of
Dooliyaanah TOAD MANSION of course
Guilty as charged.......Guilty! Guilty! Guilty!
For being insolent and committing incredulous a crime
As refusing to accept what we call crime of guilty pleasures
And hiding them away from the prying eyes of judgement
Like a secret Clandestine love affair!
Called Mad over donuts wheels of cars!
Wheels Indeed! Snached of a race car
For being impertinent with the police officer
For breaking limits of the speed beyond
Negligence or level headedness
For hijacking the car
Twelve months rigorous imprisonment
For Mr Toady and such as
All his insurmountable aggravated offences
Twu-Whit-Twu-Whoot"
Whilst typed and pounded away rat-a-tat-a-tat

The case of Terror of the Highway a speechless Mr Toad
The legal secretary of court on her typewriter
What she put in words a court verdict of typed sentences
A midget mole of a specimen
She was as big as the bump of a wart
Those perrated glands behind Mr Toadies expressionless face
Who feeling very sorry for himself
Sat in a motionless stupor of pin drop silence
Sadly hanging his head down guiltily
Being admonished by the high hand of law
He learnt his inevitable sad lesson
Mr Moley, Mr Water Ratty and Mr Badger
Reminisced the poor story of the
Soldier field mouse in love with a belle
Who after war finished
Was captured by a Barbary corsair
And made to row in the galley
And when he escaped and returned home
His belle lady love mouse
'Sundaree Chachundaree' pretty Asian House Shrew
Had gone to a convent to become a nun
This they very much applied to soul worn
Mr Toady who had an exaggerated account
Of his racing adventures and blind love for
Driving cars and wheels of every sizes and types
Even at the expense

Of losing his lady love Dotty
Over his car racing sentences and court verdicts
Who still waited for him patiently
Though not in a convent
But in her well protected fortress
Known by all to be the wealthy
Daughter of the Baron and Baroness
Toads 'The Grimmwaulds', Toadess
Dotty Grimmwauld would have to wait
If not a century but for a year
To await a changed Mr Toady
"A MR TOADY IN A SOUP BOWL!
IN A TOAD SOUP INDEED!"
They grimaced to each another!
Mr Toad in a hot soup bowl
Looking tongue tied and speechless....
In a comical sort of way
The gaoler a large sized wild Ferret
Or the Prison warden marched him up to the
Barred, barricaded and gridded tiny prison room

IN THE MEANTIME IN THE WOODS THE SAND PIPERS WHISTLE

Mr Moley was waiting for Mr Water Ratty
To arrive at his Mole end
He had promised to assist him with
Baking a fresh tray of nankatai's
Snow button biscuits
And to roll out a few marzipans and kulkuls
For the Christmas Festivities
Though couldn't keep his mind off
The sad outcome of Mr Toady's rash
Infatuation of race driving cars
And irresistible temptation
Of carjacking that led to his imprisonment
"Tut Tut", tut-tutting to himself like a King TUT TUT!
All the time muttering
"O' I guess now the cold mansion
Of Mr Toady's will be totally abandoned
Cold and cheerless
We should all arrive at a conclusion
To safe guard the place
Before it surmises to further complications
By those conniving vixens and foxes
Loitering around its bend
Hoping to capture it like a bunch

Of hooligans expecting to make a prey
Out of a beast's well laid out scheming plan"
Just then Mr Water Ratty knocked
On the door above the Mole Hole
And soon Mr Moley scurried
On his nimble feet upwards to open the door latch
And let Mr Water Ratty inside
He had just finished the batter
Of the biscuits and now had kneaded
The dough and brought out long
Combs to shape the kul-kulo's
And rat, mole, badger, frog
Funny faery animal moulds for marzipans
"What took you so long?"
Mr Moley said to Mr Water Ratty
Mr Water Ratty after a soul searching
Moment feeling very sorry for his dear
Friend Mr Otter addressed his dear chum Mr Moley
"O' dear Moley
Mr Otter insisted that I have dinner
Before I left, and such as the sorry situation
Demanded I had to keep him company
For the old fellow was worried about
His young son Tommy
He disappeared from home
Not ever showing signs of returning home anytime

Soon over the last couple of days
Now it seems to be over a good many
Four nights since his absence
And Mr Otter is sick with worry"
"O' dear" Mr Moley exclaimed in surprise
Then added
"Tommy had always the spirit of adventure
And sometimes took a day or two to come
Back home
Do you think he will be soon back home again
After his long adventures?"
Mr Water Ratty shaking his downtrodden head
Solemnly said
"Not if we try to put pieces of his straying
Together and come out with a solution
To find the chap
Maybe take out our scull boat and oars
To the spot of the back waters
He usually loved to go there
Amidst its vast surrounding flowers and perfumes
And dip his head into the fresh clear waters
That one could see even their tails and flippers
Into its clear reflection
Crystal transparent waters
I think we should at once
Scull our way to its destination"

Mr Moley fully agreed and decided
The Christmas sweet preparation
Could wait till the next morning
But now the chill of the terror night
Of losing poor Tommy
In the dark livid backwaters
And the overwhelming worry what he may face
And where may he be stranded
Robbed colour from cheery faces of two mates
They dressed in their breeches
And warm woolly gears
Carrying their pistols and a few
Handy tools like knives and hammers
Ropes and hooks
Mustering up pluck took on the cudgels
To save young Tommy and summed up in one word
Their brave venture as 'A Christmas Spirit of Tommy'
Summoning the ghosts of the backwaters
They set out on a search
To find Mr Otter's son

As they reached the Soda Inlet Bay side
And settled inside with sculls into their boat
They listened rapt to the scurrying feet on sandy banks
Sound of the sandpipers and their beautiful pipes
A contradiction of them took off

In the dark foreboding sky
Towards I guess the backwaters
Piping their merry flutes
Into the still chasm of the scented
Surrounding of nature's own green thumb
Orchard trees, crab-apple, wild cherry
And sloe
Whilst the large red moon
From under the horizon
Was pulled as if by invisible strings like a ghost puppet
Moon face mannequin
(marionette faery globe manikin)
Looming over the entire seascape
As a picturesque blob of immense blood clot harlequin face
They started sailing singing the Lord's song Kumbaya

Kumbaya my Lord, kumbaya
Kumbaya my Lord, kumbaya
Kumbaya my Lord, kumbaya
Oh Lord, kumbaya

Someone's singing Lord, kumbaya
Someone's singing Lord, kumbaya
Someone's singing Lord, kumbaya
Oh Lord, kumbayah

Someone's crying Lord, kumbaya
Someone's crying Lord, kumbaya
Someone's crying Lord, kumbaya
Oh Lord, kumbaya

Someone's praying Lord, kumbaya
Someone's praying Lord, kumbaya
Someone's praying Lord, kumbaya
Oh Lord, kumbaya

Oh Lord, kumbaya
Oh Lord, kumbaya
Oh Lord, kumbaya
Oh Lord, kumbaya

In moments of harmony and unity
Unanimously in agreement Oh Lord Kumbaya!
Alongst their blessed sculling journey
Hoping their prayers would soon be answered
Whilst watching the harlequin moon pantomime
Her fingers over her mouth like a flute play over
Thunderbird of skies grey, black, ginger and beige
With a persimmon undertone
Saturating the sky with a fresh coat of paint
Full of silvery grey and black sand pipers
Also them peering at the silent tiny hamlet
Beside the edges of the shore side
And the busy call of mating by some creatures
Of sky, surf and turf
Just brought about a sad soul searching
Note for Mr Moley and Mr Water Ratty
Trying to make sense out of the disturbing
News that recently filled
Their hearts like the sad melancholy melody of

Whistles and coos
The soothing Kumbaya praise to King
And the Pied pipers flute
Suddenly they saw the magic sand pipers
As they disappeared reappeared again
Just encircling above their heads
And playing music beautifully
As if they were trying to tell them
A secret
The backwaters were soon visible
And the place was filled with
Beautiful scent of an amazing field
Of nameless flowers
Some of them they recognized
Were sansevieria, roses, tulips
Hyacinths, dahlias and buttercups
As if relayed out of a dream
What they would now witness
Would shock them out their senses
And bring out the true soul worthy
Gift of forgetfulness of misery and woe
And gratitude to a demigod
Who wished to help them on
Their good search
And come out with a fruitful outcome
Because they dared to try to help

Poor old Mr Otter
Keeping it concealed till the special hour should come
And with the hour those who
Were called and chosen like the eight Beatitudes
By Jesus (Mathew 5:3-12)
Their selfless duty to be saviours and
To be saved
Embarking again and crossing over
They worked their way up the waters
To a silent silvery shivery forest
In a silver kingdom surrounded
By hedges, hollow trees, the runnels
And their little culverts
The ditches and dry water ways

In silence they landed
And pushed ahead through the scented
Herbage and underground
That led up to level ground
Till they moored their scull boat
And ventured out into the silvery phosphorescence
Towards the flowery margin
Of the island
The backwater banks filled quietly
Its surface above with twirling eddies
And floating foaming streaks

Deadened all other sounds
With its soothing rumble
And circling clashes of spurts
Breaking into gnashes of sea splinters
Churning, hissing and chasing Sssssss.....
One after the other big bold wavy
Currents that splashed and oozed
Instantly and gushed out spontaneously
With another on the way like incessantly babbles or gossips
Faery folk monotonously chuntered and chunnered
The waves like snails uncoiling and emerging again
Their shells or tortoises into their carapaces!
That propelled forward
The boats and waves in a rabbit tortoise race
The small island lay anchored
Fringed closely by a peripheral amphitheatre
Filled with whispering willows
And murmuring Silver Birches and alder
Reserved and shy like pretty poppet's filled with
Secrets like the game of Chinese Whispers
Both friends felt a deep consciousness
That they were finally nearing the end
The sandpipers with their gay whistles
Had vanished again
And soon when they started to plod
Through the island

They saw them circle over a strange sight
They marvelled to beheld
They saw a demigod
Truly no words could describe
Such an unearthly creature as this
It had a stag face and looked so human or god like
With a supple large behemoth body
And hooves that could gallivant Santa on his sleigh
All by himself
Was in no other way a normal reindeer
But an enormous gigantic one
And soon leaped and bounded
And then strangely stood still
A Paean describing Natures Lulling Light Display
Aurora Borealis
Appeared like an aureole of luminous jumbling
Streaks and shades of iridescent glow
Of beautiful rainbow colours- a splendid VIBGYOR
Violet, indigo, blue, green, yellow, orange and red
Just above the halo of the Paprika sundown gigantic reindeer
It was truly spectacular and rarest appearance
Of a vibrant faery dawn of truth and light
Over ignorance and darkness in the tinged painted skies
The sandpipers whistle returned
Once more its melody filled the miraculous atmosphere
High above the place where the stag bounded atop a craggy cliff

Was beckoning them to it with the sweet flute call of sand pipers
They strode through the grass ferns and tall blades
And curious amalgam of scented flower beds, weeds and thistles
Gaining speed and momentum over its rocky terrain
Ratty and Moley quickly made way farther ahead
To reach the rock face of the Heavenly Stag Horn's hoofs ground
They recalled how much Mr Otter loved his son Tommy
And was so proud of the fact
That he had taught him how to swim
And experience the joy of catching his first few fishes
Now they were coming to the final
Verdict by the Demigod of Santa Claus
A gift they would cherish forever
For the endearing Beatitudes of Christ Kingdom
Mr Moley, Mr Water Ratty and their friends
Compassing their joyous end only through faith
A Christmas Present for Tommy
A Gift of Hope, Love and Joy
That they would spread
Till it brought a smile upon the sad
Otter's face once more
Rejuvenated with the spirit of Love
This Christmas Season they would
Always remember
And from far soon they saw a pudgy figure

Of a small young Otter
Crouching fearfully yet happily
To see the friends of his father
And joyously flapping his way
To their direction
They wrapped their arms lovingly around
The mischievous one
And the glow on their cheeks
Could never be forgotten
The Demigod soon vanished
As if it flapped his wings and flew
Riding a Santa Sleigh that was invisible
To naked eye
To reveal its wisdom to humanity
That its faery folk bore witness to!
To the call of the wild wood
And Whispering Willows by the
Soda Bay inlet riverside chasm
Then Water Ratty, Moley along with dear Tommy
Returned to their scull boats
That shone white and blue
In the silvery phosphorescence
They quickly steadied their oars
And sailed back to Mr Mole's End
Hoping the next day to surprise
Their dear Old friend Mr Otter's family

With the hope of resurrection!
Wiping tears from his sodden moist black eyes!
To shed light in the dark quelling all doubts and queries
Their strange adventure, Tommy's whereabouts
And their holy encounter with the mammoth winged
Santa Sleigh Rudolph Antelope!

PRISON

MR TOADY'S ADVENTURES

Mr Toad revelled in the absconding
Escapism of having no confrontations
At all with Sergeant of Police Hound Baskerville
Judge of Owlets, jurors a flight of fancy birds
Of feathers that flocked together
And soon materialized into a compellingly
Absorbing tale betwixt him
The jailor and his pretty little daughter
Changing the result of his sordid fate
What would next culminate
In a Prism cell
No better than a dark and dinghy
Musty and hollow dungeon
As if a prey of a giant spider
Or prayer before an immense dragon
He lay prostrate before it
Consuming him in a tangled fiery web
Fully filling him with worry, woe and anticipation
Hoping to see sometimes
Through bars of the barricade
Like in a mirage of a sandy desert
His unfaltering hazy vision of
His gutsy, trusty and soulful mates
Mr Water Ratty, Mr Moley and Mr Badger

Reappearing as always in times of trouble
By tolerating every ounce of mischief
In his bones and muscles
He lambasted and berated out loudy
Rebuking his foolhardiness
To spoil his name and status
At Toady Hall
Turning him totally powerless a mite
To be pitied
All because of a silly car hijacking
In other words the very act of
Borrowing a handsome motor car
And speeding on the highway
Further away
Into the call of the wild woods
He called himself
"Stupid Stupid silly animal"
And just couldn't guzzle
The impractical salt less soups
Of cabbages or cauliflowerets
Though prepared by the gaolers daughter
A pretty, kind and generous soul she was
Whilst he languishing like a purple gnat or gnu
Inside the tongue of a lolling lady pink slipper
Of a beautiful bewitching lady urn pitcher plant prison
He idly sat squatting down to his knees

Flicking up flies and giant moths
With his slick oily tongue
That came fluttering by through bars of the dim lit
Dungeon windows
And whiled away the listless hours
Mumbling in sad sorrow
"O' dear Toady Toady Toady"
Pitying himself sorely begruntled
And thinking of the useless trouble
He'd got himself into
Sighing to himself
"Good old Mr Badger
Wise old Mr Moley
Kind old Mr Water Ratty"
Again and again
As if he was exercising
Lines like a sort of a mimicking parrot
Memorising to speak by heart
Sick with hard lessons he learnt of a gruelling prison
Meant for reforming criminals and juvenile thieves
With early morning squatting
And rigorous training spells intermittent through the day
Touching toes, spreading arms, straddling feet
Jogging, jumping and push ups
Not to say flicking fleas and jerking into hops and
summersaults

To aim tongue in cheek till practice makes perfect
He heard a Squawk somewhere in
The background
It was the Gaoler's daughters
Pet African Grey Parrot, Romeo screeching away
"Little Prison
Has caught the thief
And Little Gretel is so sweet"
Little Gretel the gaoler's daughter
Took to cooking for the old Toad
His scrumptious supper and dinners
And was worried by the weight
Mr Toady had lost in the recent
Days of his imprisonment not having any inclination
To taste her superior stews
Steamed rice and curries
Pickled gherkins with mango, eggplant and lime chunks
Potato mash, gorgonzola dressing and Dil salad
Sometimes delectable dessert flies in sundae or fondues
Especially for sad Mr Toady
She had a love for pets
And found it very hard to digest
Upon seeing poor rich Toady
Wasting his precious hours
In a grimy old prison
She thought to herself

Stroking her bald beaver
A pup Gopher as light as a feather
Moustache Parakeets Charlie Brown and Alice Liddle
With black moustaches, Weasel and a little Gerbilly
Gretel the golden ferret
Was as slender as a dreamy water nymph
Bulky and immense as a mountain of stone
All the critters surrounded
Her in a bright ring of a magic faery circle
She could sit inside and make her wishes
Turn true as if in a faery ring of magical mushrooms
She always hid them in a
Little yellow basket she carried everywhere with her
Covering over them a warm blanket
Then made up a poem of her eccentric grandfather
Ferret Michael Devasia Mathai Herbage she compared
To an Ape from Mars and herself to an opera singer
In her dream she prided to become one day

TEA
JAM

"THE OPERA SINGER FERRET AND THE GRANDFATHER FERRET APE FROM MARS"

Gretel the golden haired ferret
As dainty and slender as a reed
Of a water nymphet
Bulky and immense as a mountain of stone
Boulders of the rivers of reverie and day dreams
Of an Opera Singer from Moons Planets and Stars
Serenaded to her pup Gopher as light as a feather
As small as a dot and a tail of the weathers
She sang Orpheus a tune for better
Of her dear old Grandfather Ferret Michael Devasia Mathai Herbage
Who practiced to be a stupid moron Indeed!
Nothing more nor less than
Learning to be like an Ape from Mars
In his striped Pyjama pantaloons
And shirt made of herbs
For the herbivores
Dil, parsley, Tarragon, chervil
Thyme, Rosemary, Basil, Marjoram
Oregano

All tales inside his scullery pantry
He practised to preach never to sin
With his coloured bottles of Taboo he mastered the Ayurvedics
Like a holy Saint named St Michael Herbage Archangel
And to stroke the cue ball
So that it hit two balls in succession
As fast as a famous Billiard Player Michael Herbage Pereira the Great
Even to hit a ball in a hole with a club
Golfer like her little pet pup Gopher
With a comma and tail like a semicolon Punctuation Mark

Grandfather Ferret
The ape from mars started his work
In the wee midnight hours
On a bicycle that could GodBlimey Fly in the blooming sky!
With its sprockets, wheels and winged appendages
Gearbox, bells and horns made a desperate appeal
Granmama from right below
To come home with secret of longevity and a span of life
To never turn old, creased or sour
Like an orange, grapefruit, tangerine or pomelo
By the dozens in baskets he carried from pixels far beyond
A planet named Youth for everyone who wished to taste
Youth so Blackbeard and Black berries

From a Granpaw Greybeard and his golden bicyclette
To be supple as Eggnog of a flipper Madhatter Eggstine Einstein
His father Ferret gymnast and juggler who n'er aged by far
As his bottles of practice met with success and secret of ancient
Pearls of Wisdom and Peris of Divinity
Called Vaidya Preservatives and Occult Mystery
The Shlokas and Shastras 'Namaste' of Ancient Indian History
A secret he divulged to all in his Hamlet
To free of their bondage, futile babbage soups and baggage's of garbage
Dear Grandfather Michael Devasia Mathai Herbage of Herbivores!

He squeezed juice from all fruits
And Lemon peels called squash of ORANGE FERRET
MAGIC CITRUS WINE AND JUICE
Even squeezed tears from those who cried to tears of joy
Peals of laughter in a lighter vein and
Sadness turned to a volcano that erupted with happiness
Old age in new bottles its recipe never declines
Any fool or dithering idiot to fast forward instead rewind
Through his sublime experience he recorded Youthfulness Rotund again
Turning back the hands of Time.... A Floribunda Floriferous Garland

And tiara for young at heart meddling
With his magical Bubbutson's buttons and capsules
In other words his tablets of ingenuity and art
Till it dawned like a sun with a green Florentine
Chopped spinach, ground nutmeg, tomatoes stewed
A soup dish on the sea bed of yolks the sunny side up
Glistening with a dash of salt and pepper
Or a sliver of moony King Ombrolliet's silver omelette story
To confab and converse.........
Roundels of onions, chilly, garlic and fenugreek
To play with fork and spoon
Sun and moon nifty games with sunshine golden goose
Queen Juliet that all Humpty Dumpty King Ombrolliet's
Horses and men stuck fast to her feathers of gold
Soon releasing her golden eggs of splendour
A good omelette of nine handsome
Eggs her grandsons and grandaughters
Sometimes ham, bacon and salami to go together
With Weevil beetle loafers
They got along like bread, jam and butter
Or cheese and cold cuts
A string of sausages and meat loaves in jest!

Indeed her Grandfather Mr Ferret Michael Devasia Mathai Herbage
Tried to dip a finger in the pie

And all his fingers into different pastries and jams

Scones, tarts and cheesecakes

Like a Jack of All Trades but a Master at none

By far subjects ranging from Physics, zoology

Botany, Chemistry and Mathematics

To near sighted Philosophy and Micro Biology

To suit his palate of a varied tongues

A pinch of sodium they call Salts of Earth

For tasting purposes I suppose

In his wee chamber like a chimera

Changing hue from black

Lemon, yellow and blue to

A sunset so orangey and golden

Like the funny Ape from Mars

He straightened his posture and propellers

To the annoyance of Grandma Ferret Mary Rose Magdalene Herbage

With her apron full of splashes of

Mediterranean quiche, Quinoa salad and

Zucchini Tarts..... She guzzled with Red Rosé or white sparkling wines

All within four walls of his invention Lab

There were funny creatures

Of nonsensical lands

Like Toads, Moles, Badgers and Beavers
March Hares, Bunnies, Stoats
Possums, racoons, shrews, voles
Foxes, Vixens, Weasels and flying squirrels
All waiting to climb up
His many made up ingenious hierarchy ladders
Spires, domes, canals
Castles and towers
And up his grandfather's pendulum clock
Which was too big for the shelf
So it stood ninety years on the floor
Taller by half than the old ferret himself
CLICK-CLOCK TICK-TOCK
Ninety years without fumbling
His life a seconds numbering
CLICK-CLOCK TICK-TOCK
But it stopped, short, never to go again
When the old ferret died
All built inside his little wee lab chambers
Of experimenting
He practiced with them
And trained them for hours
Like his lab specimen artists
Where he lived in a rural village of Alonda
In a lofty Bungalow no 79
The kings, queens and varied parodies

Of his little nonsensical Hamlet
Had different personalities
Each so different than the others
And tried to fit in like puzzle pieces of a Jigsaw
With their obtuse and acute charismas
Sometimes Perpendicular as Right Angled Magicians
Performing the Black Arts
Many hats under one roof of different sizes and shapes or colours

Sighed the golden haired ferret to Mr Toadie
Higgledy Giggledy Piggledy
All footloose and fancy free
Tried chasing a Pussycat
As large as a goat on a map
They hailed a flight upon a unicycle bike
And fit all in Grandfather's
The Ape from Mars shoulders and lap
Climbing and distributing his branches of degree of Philosophy
With their scholarships and graduate caps
Raced as they wheeled on feet instead
Like tiny tots of nursery kindergarteners
Sparking electric circuits
By pitter-patter of feet
Right as rain indeed
Over trains, pyramids, sphinxes

Roves and buses on wheels
Scooters, bikes and Lorries
They skidded.......Skedaddle doo!
Skedaddle Skid! And stopped at traffic signals
And like children raced pitter patter
On legs rolling further onwards

Sometimes ferrying their boats with oars
A jamboree of lab specimen
For play therapy in a play room
Behind the tiger pussy cat
All followed like in a circus pandemonium
Hoisted a flag and belled the pussycat finally
In the tiny wee chamber of four walls
And the nonsensical rhymes soon rhymed
Of the opera singer golden haired ferret
As dainty and slender as a reed
Of a water nymphet
Bulky and immense as a mountain made of stone
Boulders of the rivers of reverie and day dreams
Of an Opera Singer from Moons Planets and Stars
She serenaded to her pup Gopher as light as a feather
As small as a dot and a tail of the weathers
She sang Orpheus a tune for better
The melody traversed afar
Up towers, down babbling brooks

With funny rocks and stones
As huge as boulders to building blocks
For a writer Sophie a script made up
Full of slime, moss, lichen and froth
Down its hills, toadstools
Vales, Dales and valleys in the middle
Of a little lotus and lily pond
Where the opera singer golden haired ferret
Tired to droll, loll her pink tongue and sing her song
Of the story of the wild wooded throngs

Clapping her hands together "Hurrah! Hurrah!"
Pleased at making an attempt at Poetry and Arts
Having a shot at reciting it
Like a great Scholar of Reverie and Day dreams
Little Gretel's inseparable pets like Dorothy and Toto
Of Wizard of Oz!
She like Babes in the Wood
Hansel and Gretel
Working in a witches ginger bread prison
Broiling, stewing, churning milk
Into yoghurt and making cheese
Baking pizzas in ovens and stirring up
Cock-a-leekie soup in her huge magic cauldron pot
For a good three hundred prisoner
Stoats, foxes, peevish meeces, hares

Barbaric porcupines with sharp pin prickle
Bristles that were punished for squatting
Along with their poky relatives
Inside an old property, squatters to their core
Bamboozlers, embezzlers and every tricksters of con
Artists and connivers
Storks, monkeys and cranes
Even tortoises, squirrels, rabbits and tiny quails
She treated as her very own pets and sweethearts
And fed them with whatever
Rations were given to her
To prepare food for the prisoners inside
Like fruits and vegetables, sunflower and pumpkin seeds
To her birds of flight
Whilst Mr Toady rationed out
What little was left in his imagination
At this sorry instance
Captured in a strange dungeon
Remembering every spoonful
Of the thick cream of mushroom soup
Beef stroganoff, Italian Minestrone
Salt and peppered ox tongue
With parsley rich creamy sauce
Tartar sauce with fish fingers
Chicken Ala King, Gazpacho (a fresh cold soup
Made of cucumbers and tomatoes), Pear and Gorgonzola salad

Peppercorn sauce and roast beef
All prepared lovingly by cheeky chef
Mr Nuttles the honest Beaver
Even sometimes fleeting thoughts about
His dear lovelorn admirer Toadess
Dotty Grimmwauld daughter of
Baron and Baroness Mr and Mrs Grimmwauld
The prudent owners of the saucy business
Of ham and strings of sausages to go with them
Not to say the wealth and luxury that he basked to glory of his
Great Great Great Grand Uncle's heritage mansion passed on
To him 'The Great Toad Hall'
Doo Dahling Dooling Dooliyaanah Mansion
That he missed so much
Even his dear animal faery farm folks
The beaver, tortoises, pig sties
Sheep pen, hens, cocks, bulls
David his dear horse of the old caravan
And his horse stables
The stoat, dogs, cats and the weasel
His white mice, pheasants and the turkeys
All sadly he lost that once dearly he cherished
Little Gretel her long tresses of gold
Fell right to her pink rubicund glowing cheeks
Wherefore asking her father the gaoler's permission
To attend to poor little grieving

Mr Rich Toady like his Faery God Child
She was allowed to do so by her crusty
Irritable old father wild ferret the gaoler
Like an old cantankerous crabby man
Who after taking great liberties
To Mr Toady's fat wallet lined with dollars and cents
For providing him with some fine luxuries
Like bed linen and food
Or maybe rashers of ham and bacon
With poached eggs
The reason being that he couldn't bear
To see his daughter mop
Over the poor animal
As soon as the golden sunshine girl, little Gretel
Entered the small and musty miserable chamber
With a plate of toast buttered
Sizzling with golden dabs of butter
A spread of sweet pineapple jam
Then he rose from his squat position
With its honeyed whiff
Like a bee to a nectared flower
Rather pulled like a magnet
To sweet and golden haired pretty little Gretel
A shiny little Buttercup Ferret Faery
And stood up to greet the little girl with a bow and curtsy
Gretel had tears in her eyes

To see the Handsome and Charming
Kind and benevolent soul
Suffer so terribly in prison days
Then offering her his handkerchief
To wipe away his tears
He started to sob and whimper
Crying bucketfuls of watery tear drops
Like a little grown up boy all over the shoulders
Of the well mannered and thoughtful
Gaoler's daughter who possessed 'Magic Hands'
Comforting the sorrow stricken toad
With her soft and loving strokes
Mr Toady complained about his sorry life in prison
And his happy bygone hey days
Back at Toad Hall Mansion
She offered to wipe his streaming tears
That had saturated his stamina as much
His undernourished weary body could take
Showing upon his gaunt face and hollowed cheek bones
And then offering him the plate
Of buttered toast with pineapple jam
Patted poor old Toady
Addressing him as her Uncle she said
"Dear Uncle Toady
My father the gaoler told me
About your craze for driving handsome

Cars steer wheels and helms of boats of any and every kind
Don't worry you learnt a sad lesson indeed
And now I surely will help you escape
The dungeon of darkness"
"O' Dear Soul"
My dearest girl Gretel
Light at the end of a tunnel at last!"
Mr Toady rejoiced reading her name
From the badge pinned to
Her grey pinafore and white blouse
As if she was a student of a high school
And he an unfortunate Master Professor Toad
Rather a washer woman in distress
Who he would soon turn into with some help from
Such a nice Ferret Maiden of honour
He always desired to meet
Such a kind and gentle soul
And now not containing any more of his joyous outbursts
He whispered in her ears a great jubilant cry
"I am WHOOP WHOOOOOPIE DO DE DOO!
So happy, happy as can be how can I ever
Express my gratefulness to you
What kind of mess is this?
That I have landed myself into
I will definitely shower upon you
A hundred dollar note

If you only tell me how
And in which manner this would
Be possible
To exit this hideous dungeon
O' how remorseful I am for my deeds
I guess no one can fully comprehend"
Then the girl adjusting her apron
On her grey and white uniform
Went on to whisper in her Uncle Toady's ear
"My aunt is a washerwoman here
Her name Jennifer
And she is the kindest soul
Her figure is almost your size"
Mr Toady quite insulted at her funny comment
Went on to say
"I don't think so my dear I do have
A very aristocratic nose and lean body
Much like a T.... I...mmean TV Tarzan!
Rippet Rippet"
He meant V when hardly so
And looked like an honourable Tee
Or super exaggerated TV Tarzan extraterrestrial toady
With telepathic receptors or antennae
One could really notice at the ends of his funny
Face with its aristocratic humbug nose
Then the little girl Gretel getting

Annoyed with his impertinence replied
"You lost rich souls
Are all the same
You cannot understand
The meaning of tolerance
Rich uppity classes
All I meant to say
Is you will have to act
And behave like a WASHER WOMAN
Mrs Jennifer my aunt
And she is beautifully bulky
Or even when you say how
You shall exit this doomsday dungeon
Do you expect to travel like
Cinderella in a Pumpkin coach
With mice horsemen
And frog liveries?
I suggest you should take the next
Train out this daggone country
Once you are out of the Prison gates"
She sarcastically jeered at the Uncle Toady
"Better be able to accept
Modestly the role that I ask you
To act out or else you'll be languishing
In the dungeon for twelve months
And not to say missing out all those things

You love, your friends and Toad Hall you cry and cry
So much about"
Then bidding him warmly an adieu
And promising to return back
With her aunt the Washer Woman's
Poorly tatty costume the next day
Giving him a peck on his salty tear stained cheeks
Little Gretel the Gaoler's daughter took leave

Mr Toady dreamed the night
How he always groomed himself before a party
In front a great heirloom three facetted Victorian Vanity mirror
In his royal Dudeoir (Male equivalent to Boudoir)
Generally how he would appear
And behave with charm and charismatic appeal
Before his splendid upper class audiences
Never failed the loving eye
Especially by Toadess Dotty Grimmwauld
Stealing gazes at the handsome charmer
She thought he had it all
A Five worded handsome package Mr 'G.C.W.P.H.TOAD!'
Good Looks, Charm, Wit, Personality
And humour to go along with its title like a PHD Graduate
Philosophical Hedonistic Doctor Toad!
Giving himself away in sweet abandon
He just thought about her so often nowadays

Her sweet encouraging voice
As she was floored by his clothes horse personality
In his stiff large cloaks
Short breeches and vests
Vast array of shoes, boots and galoshes that matched
Always admiring him secretly
As she used to tell him
Over a glass of wine or sherry
"Mr Toady O' how I love it
When you drive me under the moonshine
And the romance by the star way stairway
Panorama of our galaxies on one of those runway boats
Through the Whispering Willow wood and riverwaters
Like stowaways on a boat and in runway cars
You always steer
The wheel and helms and zoom me away
To a different planet
On the run every time through wild woody roads
Like your Princess Dotty
Of a faraway Kingdom
Two Doodahling Doolings
How I long to be your Mrs Dooliyaanah Little Toadess
Of Mr Dooliyaanah Little Toad
Of Dooliyaanah Mansion soon one day
Oh Mr Toady O' how I love
All the Mr 'G.C.W.P.H.TOAD' attention you shower
Aww Shucks! You do make me blush!"

She said it as if she were all dotty over Mr Toadie
A replica reincarnation of his spotty loony uncle
Mr Dooliyaanah Little Toad
"A blast of horn from the past"
I suppose he smiled ear to ear blushing coyly
But gradually the boyish wide grin
Changed to a long old grimace
From mouth to chin
"O' Poor Me
Now I will have to act
Like an old natty Washer Woman
And God Knows! What the men folk
Should have to say to me
Maybe warm and snuggle up
Roughen up to their thick bulky shoulders before I leave"
Being wary of the advantage they
Took of little older ladies
Especially an eccentric washer woman
Like Golden Ferret Gretel's Dotty Aunt Jennifer
Giving steely Lizard watch guards little hugs and pecks
Before she left her work place
And a sweet kiss upon their foreheads and cheeks too!
Praying deep down his heart he'd give the correct
Answers to the clouts and clowns before he left
The forsaken dungeon at last
Into the wilderness!

Then next day Little Gretel
Brought her bright yellow basket
This time instead of her darling pets it contained
Few strawberries she'd plucked from
Her garden and a bowl
Of bland mutton bones stew
She heartily had prepared for her Dear Uncle Toadie
Along with a few clothes
He'd have to wear and behave
As the odd Washer Woman aunt
That Kind little Golden Ferret Gretel
Stole into the prison cell
Early at dawn
Before anyone could notice
As her aunt only arrived late morning
After she had taken care of the laundry, washing
Drying and ironing
Was expected to leave late after lunch dressed
In her Coat, Bonnet, Dress, Muffler, Scarf
Mittens and flowery apron
Looking at her matronly clothes Toady remarked
"Only a good hide for grandmother wolf"
"Awhooooo......woof woof!" He barked comically
As she exchanged it with his overcoat
Waist coat pocket and breeches
She chortled out a funny laugh

As if she couldn't get over
Mr Toady as the Stooge Washer Woman
Mr Toady briskly crawled under her skin
As if he pulled a rabbit out of a hat
So well like an actor or a magician
As he had improvised his lines
And dialogue the night before
As soon as the Lizard guards
Noticed her leaving after brunch
They seized the opportune moment
To chit chat before they could open
The gates of the prison
And she could exit the stage
Now taking on the voice of an elderly woman
Mr Toady started to speak very funnily
Though it really did not sound like what
An uncivilized Washer Woman would say
"Now I've gone loony with the chaff
I mean surf and sapp (soap bubbles)
And the rest of the linen"
As he nervously giggled whilst saying his lines
Then continuing outrageously spiel of comic stanza next
He rhymed poetry
Bowing a curtsy, pinching his skirt
And showing off a naked knee
Acting rather bold and cheeky

He ironed out his lines straight as a poker joker
"You stoats and weasels
Hares and bears
Hog and mares
Ferrets, beavers and mice
Officers and partners in crime
I've dried out on clothes lines and pegs
Burrp Hic....Pegs Ahem! Pigs I mean........I mean clothes pegs"
He she (Toadie) chuckled
"Every linen ironed out and folded neatly
I have surfed out the sponges
And cleaned out the longes (long Johns)
The prison breeches and dirt on collars even stenches
Foul now without a slightest odour
I've washed and rinsed
Like I am totally
Like a mop squeezed out"
Well as hardened criminal lizard guards
They burst into squeals of laughter
As well retorting back crudely
At her poetical outburst of a song
She sung like a melody
Laughing a riot amongst themselves
"Ha Ha Ho Ho Hum Haw
What a loony toony washer woman
Of a mop squeezed out"

With loud guffaws and jibes
At the poor woman none other than
Comical stooge Mr Toady of Toad Hall Mansion
The officer hoodlums brashly commented
"We didn't know you learnt
To sing poems
Like a scholar would say jokes
On a Washer Woman chores"
Mr Toad calmly retorted to the rowdy Lizard jesters
A cock and bull story which was certainly
True only in Toad Hall washroom
By all respected Toads and family
"O' I turned bathroom singer
Washing linen all the time
I just couldn't show it to the children"
She I mean Mr Toady in disguise
Joked at the rascals punning
"Wouldn't you want my farewell kiss?"
And secretly sickened with the revolting idea
Of sparing such fools a faery kiss
'Fools rushing in where angels fear to tread'
Fancying himself wearing a writer's foolscap
Meant for the Angels of Venus from their mercy seat
To shower upon everyone their sweet kisses
Like the loony washer woman from Mars
Supposedly that Mr Toady donned a Dunce cap upon her head

For giving away angel's kisses
For y'see the dotty washer woman Jennifer had always
Reserved them a naughty kiss
Before she left the prison gates
The little secret told by her niece Gretel
The rogues of Lizard officers not sparing
Washer woman Mr Toad in disguise remarked cheekily
"Now then surely would we not ask
For a Coochicoo kiss like you usually
Do before you leave"
"Do unto others as you do to yourself"
Toady pacified whispering to himself secretly
"Do and do, so and so
Here I go to fly a faery kiss
With my faery wings
High above the prison gates!"
He had practised
A fly kiss in his dream in front
Of his heirloom three facetted Victorian Vanity Mirrors
Then spitting out on the ground
With much despise
He smiled again so that they couldn't see
His strong revolt and disgust to cover up his mocks
"Cheee.....Awwkkkk.....Yuckkk...."
The forbidden kiss of the faery task he had to perform
Bravely shinning up he extended his knees

And bulky draped washer woman body
Encircling his arms around their necks
Giving a kiss like a frog prince
To each of the two tall Lizard officers
Or patrol guards on their stretchy
Reptile skin dewlaps and burning dry scaly cheeks
And a matronly cuddle
Shoulder to shoulder
Mr Toady assessed the danger
As if in mortal combat of betrayal with kisses and hugs
"'T would be he she or they"
Mr Toady concluded to himself
Losing self on the battlement rather bafflement of his disguise
After a smashing performance
Pinching his little dress and apron up
He was in for a pleasant surprise in the end of a very
Dark tunnel
At last there was LIGHT!
Then he heard the wicket gate
In the great outer door click behind him
He heaved a sigh of relief
And the riff-raff of the chaff audience
Stern Lizard police men disappeared from sights
As if the strange nightmare had ended
He soon ventured out late afternoon
By a narrow lane in the direction of the train station

He heard the chug chugging
Of the chugging steam engine train
"A-ha Luck Almighty! Luck at last!"
Hoping to remove Three cents
For the ticket to Toad Hall
From his pocket strings
However he realised he had
Forgotten to remove the thick lined wallet
From his waist coat pocket leaving also
His long overcoat, breeches, chained clock
All in the hands of Miss Gretel
"O"' sighed Poor Mr Toady
"No money at all to pay
For my train ride
Anytime now the Chef of Police
And the rest officers
Will come looking for me
I have to duh....think of something quick"
Then he saw an old strict straight postured Rooster
Get inside with a crocodilian of baby chick Kindergarteners
Holding an immense foot ruler to correct them
Hesitating he began to beg
Before the old teacher maybe the Principal
In the voice of the good old washer woman
"Please Please dear Mr Rooster
Could you give me your ticket?

I have lost all my possessions
And have no money to travel
I need to get home
And prepare a meal for my old husband
You see my grandchildren are
O' dear too small to handle his dire needs
Cooking his dinner
And giving his medicines on time
And my married daughter her husband
Ran away with a weasel
She is heart broken and can't handle family"
"Ehh..." the stern old Mr Rooster
Replied to Mr Toady
"Get away Washer Woman
And let the children pass"
Snidely remarking "You poor lady"
Mr Toady hated the comment
And was thoroughly miffed by the rude Rooster
"He surely could have spared his ticket to washer woman
I mean Mr Toady" thought overwhelmed Mr Toad
In his poor dizzy dazed head
As big drops of tears fell on his cheeks one by one
It could fill a huge washing tub
The Pussycat engine driver on the way to the engine room
Luckily spotted the Washer Woman lady
Bawling out loudly

And began to question her quiet innocently
"What may the matter be?
Dear Little Lady
Could I be of any help?
You seem to be the washer woman of the prison"
He recognised the scarf, bonnet, flowery apron
And matronly Dress which was given only to the Prison
Washer woman who travelled daily by his car engine
Because the Pussycat engine driver
Had an immense handlebar moustache
That twirled upwards like curvy ribbons
Mr Toady addressed him as Mr Pussycat Handlebars
Mr Toady tried to hammer out
The same story
About his husband being very old
Her heart broken daughter whose husband left her for a weasel
And his grandchildren not being able to look after
The dotty man
Playing with matches, upsetting lamps
The little innocents and quarrelling he added
And going on generally
"O' dear, O' dear me
What am I to do Mr Pussycat Handlebars?
Do let me get into the train"
The train driver befuddled
By his piteous lamentations obliged to help her out

There were only thirty minutes left
For him to strain out the coals
Into the furnace of the old train
Saying to the woman
"If only you washed my dirty linen
There" and handed over a load
From inside the cab of the engine
But Poor Toady 'twas all he could really take
And trusting the kind hearted engine driver Mr Pussycat Handlebars
Poured out his heart telling out all real truth
That in fact he was the smart and famous
Mr Toad of Toad Hall
Not the silly stooge of a washer woman he acted out to be
And had made an erroneous error
To borrow somebody else's car
In the bargain had been sentenced a rigorous imprisonment
Of twelve months
Then he rattled on
Assuming his own croaky crackling voice
"Please Please Mr Engine Master Pussycat Handlebars
Have mercy on me
I promise I've changed for the better
Let me on your train
The police would come barging after me
Any moment now and take me back

To their grizzly dungeon"
The engine driver felt very sorry for the infamous
Mr Toady of Toad Hall Mansion and told him to hop
Inside the cab of the engine
But instructed him that in some distance
After he started fuelling hot coal into the furnace
They would enter into a dark tunnel
He would make the big engine halt
And soon Mr Toady would have
To take a leap into the wild wood beyond
The engine driver knew as much the police
Would be on the next train following them
In a Thief Police chase
Behind the train that Mr Toady boarded
And started the engine just in time
Fuelling the coal into its burning furnace
Right from the oven of the car engine cab and into the fire
Rather from the fire to the furnace
And from furnace into the fire
Taking on the lashings like a scapegoat washing woman
Wash her dirty linen in public
Covered in black soot of coal dust as the steam engine
Furiously let out black smoke through its chimney
In clouds amassing above the dark sky
Naturally with a silver lining
For soon the train began to wind down

Like an immense shiny green caterpillar
Going towards a windy dark tunnel
Where soon Mr Toady would jump as instructed
By the engine master
At that very moment
He heard the Hound Baskerville Sergeant of Police
And the patrol guard Meeces storm into the station
They barged inside
Whistling with their whistles
Waving halberds
Armed in their helmets with their truncheons
Detectives like in Bond 007 with revolvers, walking sticks
And snarling blood thirsty trained bull dog hounds
It was too late the engine had begun
To rattle and roll down
With its chimney song
Chug chug chug chug a chug! At a great pace
Making its way forward
Rattling and rolling towards the dark long tunnel
As if it was aware of being pursued
By the next caterpillar steam engine following behind
Rattling its wheels on the railway tracks
Till finally it was inside the long windy
Tunnel and miserable Mr Toady
Crouching in the coal dust, stood up and waved goodbye
To the kind engine driver

From its wide door as it gently halted
He was experienced enough
To take a long triple jump
Somersaulting into the
Wild woods yonder
Still wearing the scarf
Dress, mittens and apron
Of the washer woman
He wondered to himself
How he would make it out of
The woods
When suddenly a large owl
Hooted by his shoulder making fun
A low laugh....."HO! HO! HO!"
Teasing poor old Toady's
Black sooty face and attire
Still incessantly loofing and hooting Hootininnys
"Twu Whit Twhu Whoots
HO! HO! HO!"
As if he didn't care
Two hoots what poor Mr Toady thought of it
Loofing, laughing and loafing
On slender bough of the hollow tree
Once he met a fox
Who stopped and looked
At him from head to foot

In a sarcastic sort of way
And said
"Hullo, Washerwoman
I guess you've got
My hide Grandma Grandma!
Washing somebody's dirty linen again
You should return
Grandmother her apron strings
Dress, scarf, bonnet, mufflers and mittens
Haven't you finished laundry
It's a half a pair of socks
And a pillow case short
Red Riding Hood is waiting
Mind you it doesn't occur again"
And swaggered off sniggering "HEHEHEHEHE!"
Toad looked about for a stone
To fling at the foxy creature
But could not succeed in finding one
Which vexed him more than anything
At last hungry, cold and tired
He sought shelter
Under the Whispering Willow Tree
With its dead branches and leaves
Made himself as comfortable as he could
And slept soundly till the next morning
Dawned

MIGRATING, HIBERNATING, SEA FARER'S AHOY WAYFARERS ALL AND MR WATER RATTY

Migration to green pastures and hibernation
To underground holes with
Rice, barley, oats, nuts, berries and
Conkers and capers
Filled their stacked treasuries
Of the field mice, gerbils and squirrels
For soon the winter
The ploughing and tractors
Would make way through the fields
It was time to hibernate into their
Little gaols like Prisoners
Even the birds migrated to the south shores
Their brilliant fan tails decked like a jubilee
Ready to get set and go
With a bullet shot that rang like a jarring
Disturbance by the hunters
Pointing rifles at the ducks, pheasants
And the cocks
Of the Murray fields
Most of them desired to see the south
Where the end of misery
Of the cold west would turn to green
Passports of joy and

Freeing encumbrances
All in one flight of birds of feathers flocking together
Even along the way he met the sea farer mouse
Who spoke at length about his salty sea adventures
Like Robin Hood Christopher Columbus Rat
Even a Vasco Da Gamma Portugese Rat explorer
A Great Emperor Napoleon Rat with his fleet of ships
Or Giant Gulliver Mouse travelling to the land
Of tiny Lilliputs
Who in fact was a sea faring sailor shipwrecked
And marooned on an Island
Full of midgets the size of six inches
Who at first wished to tie him with magic hops and bind weed
And starve him to death
But later rejoiced when he saved the Lilliputians
From the Blesfuscudian invasion
(A laugh indeed for so silly a battle presumably invented
Over which way would be the right side to break an egg)
Stopped in time by Giant Gulliver Mouse
By dragging the Blesfuscudian ships to Liliput
In gratitude the Emperor of Liliput
Rewarded the Brobdingnagian Gulliver
The Title of Nardac Mouse!
It all seemed a thumb puppet play of
Meeces and Rat Tales away
When the jocund sea farer mouse
Composed himself a poetic seafaring Bard of a Rat

Poetry he had made up himself
And profitably had sold many copies
Of his captivating solid illustrated sea books
About the Lilliputian goblins and the staid Rock Giant frock
That he gifted Mr Water Ratty
After removing it from his blue satchel
Painted with anchors, stars and cheesy moons
He carried everywhere a dozen copies
Of his **fabulous fantastical** poetry book with his signed autographs
.............By Sea Faring Rat
Which he always carried like a chunk
Of magic blue moon cheese and a loaf of stale bread everywhere
He usually sold them for three cents each as they
Were quite popular with young sailor meeces
Even ferret lasses and gerbillie lads
When his ship voyages touched harbour
His splendid composition on Rock Climbers
That Mr Water Ratty with his reedy spectacles
Called Grand paw's Rosy lorgnettes
Started to read out loud
Turning the pages one by one very joyously
And spooning each verse into a mountain of a mole hill
MOUTHFUL SEA SAILING ADVENTURE!
Piece by piece, stanza by stanza......

"ROCK CLIMBERS"

With rock locks, helmets
Rock harnesses, rock torch lights on heads
Ice axes, hammers, climbing ropes
Shoes, slings and haversacks
Climbed atop the zealous rock climber
Hob Goblins one by one marking with chalk
The slate gray rock

Clambered up the rocks of an old soiled ankle
Then again an old withered kneecap
With rope they lugged and hook anchored
Again to the top they scrambled menacing heights
Further and further higher to the colossal clouds
Swung from a beard long and luscious
Like shrubs bulging out from a chin
Its nooks and crevices
As they shinned up held again
A long hooked nose from up the bedraggled mossy chin
Tossed upon it a rope
Till they were quite steady
Where giant moles lay buried

They climbed further from a straggling lip
From their noose clamped to their belts

Hung from a brow bushy as hell
As a scraggy shore
Great pools appeared bright red
Like burning ruby embers
Sometimes cerise irises of pupils
So big like planets
They got bigger and bigger
Revolving inside its river beds
As they glanced staggering right into them
The dazed little hob goblins looked askance
At those rolling round and round giant planets
Bulging in their huge sockets
Reeling, contorting, writhing
Dilating and contracting

Indeed they climbed a mighty and strong
Monstrous giant
The wee hob goblins played around him
His moulded contour
An irregular outline or silhouette
Against the rising or dimming sun
Their mini farm animals
The moose, cliff goats, rams, horses and calves
Gleefully bleated, mooed, whinnied and gloated all around them
Whilst they whispered and sang songs
Mountain clef notes and shoulder cavities their bars

On their hurdy-gurdies and harmonicas
Even playing sometimes rock and roll with their guitars

Sometimes condescending the dreaded beasts
That visited such a Mountain Giant
Vultures of prey…… Bald Eaglets
The wee hob goblins
Turned them friendly neighbours instead of foes
By offering them their chicken offal's
Gizzards, livers, hearts, entrails
Even bone marrow
A few beautiful pots of their plants, creeping vines
Hibiscus, poison ivy, shamrock and ice cream flowers
Peeped from pockets
They'd keep on their window sills
Tall chimneys huffed and puffed rings of smoke
From thatched roofs of their teeny huts
Through their teeny windows
Upon his steep mountain cliff
"Alas! We've settled!"
The wee hob goblins sighed

They could see rivers, valleys, dales
Castles, tombs, cathedrals, spires, mountains
Temples, aeroplanes and catacombs
Oh what a splendid outcome

When the giant snored, snorted
Opened wide his jaws
Back again before he awoke
They scurried right into his pockets
All the three hundred tiny hob goblins
Lived right in his grassy waistcoat and scarred pant pockets

Under the bright sun furnace
Toasted toes and fingers
Huddled warmly in their coverlets, duvets and blankets
The giant's great green gauntlets
Till once again he stood like thunderous clap
Towering tall from up his withered boots
High atop his steep mountain cliffs
A precipice deep and dangerous soon fell
The funny hob goblins
From inside his tattered waist coat and pant pockets
Their huts and dwellings
Scattered about just here and there
Whilst he took a mighty dip and splash
Into a riverbed
Gushing beneath his ankles
For a routine day time scrub and wash
Now their thatched roves sailed in his pants and waistcoat pockets
"Another flood"

They sighed again, grumbled and complained
Once more the funny hob goblins
Clambered and struggled
Shinning right to the top
Trekked, wobbled and hobbled back again
Of the mountain giant's pinnacle
Right above his matted forehead
That creased with great big furrow lines

This time swung with the help of his charcoal dreadlock braids
Lunged forth
His ropes mighty and strong
Returning under shade of his sunny barmy brimmed hat
Hale and heartily once more again
He never took it off
Until the flood that threatened receded
And the giant reversed his footsteps
To stand strong a gargantuan mountain cliff
Worn out even
A few strands of his waistcoat and pant pockets
A straggling threadbare ho and a hem on its edges still
Like a boat had sailed the three hundred wee hob goblins
"Ahem!" Sighed the great big giant
"Not the tiny hob goblins again"
The tiny inhabitants of the mountain giant!

Once again populated his rocky ladder
And terrain
High up the strange mountain cliff
Did the rock climbers climb and shin up again
Living off the bread crumbs
He stored every now and then in his patchwork pockets
Fruits, cheese and meat chunks
A variety he'd keep in some
Even spare ribs, pork chops or beef fillet
Sometimes with their fishing hooks and tackles
Wee hob goblins
Ferreted and fished scrupulously
Fishes and crabs from his nearby ankles
From inside the ponds or riverside
Where his dirty mud stained galoshes dipped he

He'd love desserts this friendly giant
As big as sugared kernels
And flakes of corn
He'd pour in milk
His daily gruel
Humble porridge, homily grit and bran
Those he battered with his bludgeon
And hammered to make corn samples
Sometimes he would offer
For his tiny hamlet of wee hob goblins

Living in his day light dungeons
Working night time scullions
Prepared rare meads and luncheons
With the rock giants scraps and tit-bits!

The rock climbers
Summoned one and all
Its wee hob goblins
In the tiny hamlet
Proud of their achievements
Whilst the busy hob goblins singing a valour song
For their steep cliff mountain hero
The gargantuan Giant!
Upon his steep mountain cliff
Where they lived happily and peacefully again
Their voices reverberated, echoed and reverted back again
Their glorious song
"Hail! The mighty rock climbers
Of the mountain giant!"

Crinkled and wrinkled
His mud, grit, sand and loins
Whilst they hoisted with his own petard
The three hundred wee hob goblins
Rock climbers in search of truth and wisdom!

"We climb the rocks
To the mountain tops
And guess we live
On a giant as mighty as a Saint
Who willingly let us wee hob goblins
Dwell on his spectacular terrain!
Of his staid rock giant frock
Vales, valleys and mountain tops!"
---------Signed A Sea Faring Rat

Expressing his gratitude Mr Water Ratty
Thanked and gratefully shook
The adventurous sea farer's hands
Saying to him; "Well Done Amigo!"
The sea farer rat smiled and still continued
About his many encounters on his globe trots
Around the world
When in fact all his sea faring voyages
Began with famous explorers
Including voyagers of great examples like
Christopher Columbus, John Cabot
Samuel de Champlain
And many others to obscure foreign lands
And meeting many usurpers like British
Colonists he further rambled
About their faery like colonies he visited

Especially the land of milk and honey, India
And the vast acres of Hungary
Even Budapest along the Danube River
Turkey, Espanola and Zimbabwe
Slovenia, Slovakia and Czechoslovakia
Switzerland, Portugal and Denmark
After independence had turned to Commonwealth nations
And their rainbow flags hoisted upon their flageolet flagpoles
Their lentil tails had spread their roots
Mostly globetrotting by sailing with sailors
The tall tales of ships with Vikings and Buccaneers
He undertook like a water rat
Sea farer or a water hog of the seas
Ship ahoy!
The many anchors lowered and destinations
Mapped as would explorers do commissioned
By Royal Patronage
Brainwashed by the strange bonding spirit
Of the sea farer buccaneer rat
He thought they made such a good team together
Who at last sadly bid him a farewell adieu!
Off on his next sea faring Bon Voyage
Grimly resulted in restless Mr Water Ratty
Deciding to migrate
Like a sea farer
And sulking over losing comradeship

Of his dearest feathered plumage friends
All who had migrated into the south shores
He returned drooping, despondent and downtrodden
All set to take on his gauntlets
And oar into oblivion
Maybe to some southern shore
To be lost in tales of folklores
Like the infallible sea faring mouse
Trapped in a water bound ship
Or like a gallant explorer in his many
Explorations like a chick pea, horse gram
Or a monkey nut
Gallivanting into its unknown obscurity
Uncharted territory yonder turpentine and Galipot of blue ink
Entering through the stern end of a hatch
Down a large blue ship
Into a future that was blind to reason
Or stability
He returned to comfortable Mr Mole End's little
Underground door hatch and knocked at the top
Rat-a-tat-a-tat-knockity-knock-knock
To the very bottom of it
"Who's there?" Mr Moley asked from deep inside
"It's me" answered Water Ratty rather forlorn and dejected
Over losing his sea faring buccaneer rat companion
An old and experienced sea dog unlike a landlubber like him

All his hibernating wild wood critters
And his fanciful free flight friends
Determined to join them, if he couldn't beat them though
Soon Mr Moley appeared opening his door latch
And welcomed Mr Water Ratty
Who was trying to explain his raw gut feelings of exploration
Like the harmless birds, bees and water rat sea farer
Of migration, hibernation and sea sailing buccaneers
He had almost packed his little suitcase
Full of what little he possessed
His neat blue suit, his pink cardigans
Priceless bows, shirts and neck ties, his velvet carpet flip-flops
Leather Moccasins and huge gum boots
He had made up his mind
And explained to Mr Moley
All in a daze as if like water rat washed
And sloshed high in spirits "I'm off
Like all good restless water rats
Should be
Away on a mast and a sail
Away with oars and paddles
Away on the jesty sea"
Mr Moley surprised at the sudden
Tear jerking and over exaggerated expectations
Of Mr Water Ratty to be a Water Rat Sea Farer
Like the one he spoke about

He met on a wild rendezvous to some port excursion
On his way by the timid fields was totally flabbergasted
And pinned the creature down on all his fours
"Don't be Foolish Water Ratty
Now calm down
Nothing should make you so distressed
As news of the water bound or the migratory wayfarers
And their sailor stories
Even the herbivores and the hibernators"
Then taking off his muddy gumboots
And woolly cashmere coat
He settled him hobbling to the sofa
And made him put his feet up
Mr Water Ratty soon in a daze
Fell into a deep trance like sleep
Moaning and muttering
Strange slogans of the sea
And the sea men
"Hooray Bon Voyage
Ship Ahoy
Booyah! Cheers!"
As the anchor was lowered
And he began fantasising his unrealistic chimera
Of a big bubble blown into a sweet dream
From his restless turmoil
The changing seasons of the field trip experience!

Like a carnivore beast
Consumed by ravenous hunger the next day
The same old mouse with a voracious appetite
Of a sturdy hound canine Mr Water Ratty
Would come to his senses finally
After Mr Moley prepared him his favourite dish
Of mussels, a pot of cherry Pina-colada mock tail
And an olive Margarita cock tail
To savour with toasted prawns
And squid calamari's on tooth picks
Those Mr Otter had surprised Mr Moley
The day when Mr Water Ratty had got out
On one of his unforgettable field trips
The lulling lullaby
And the disappearing shrills
Of the migrating, hibernating and sea faring
Creatures of the Whispering Willows
Only its boughs and branches
Stirred murmurs and whispers
By the Soda Bay Inlet Beach
He would jot down with sea ink
In one of his journals
A poem that Mr Moley loved
To scribble about Mr Water Ratty
Mad rush of adrenalin
And his soaring ambition

Plunging into depths of deep waters
The Voyage of Water Rat with blue sea ink of course!
He plumbed his composition ditty

"THE VOYAGE OF THE SEA RAT"

From anon the harbours
Of pin vales and valley
Of the Great Mangy Ferocious sea Tiger Cat
And into the Galipot of Blue Ink
And Turpentine so often painted
Its slick oil paints canvas
The buccaneers
The bay of Lombardy or Barberry
The bay of Tuscany's
Set sail the sun smiling sea farer
Water ratty with oars and sculls
Sails and masts
To win the hand of his water Rat bride Abigail Cleoratra
Gushing rosy and rouge so coyly
He gritted the grin with bear and stump
He flitted the moon with oar and hump
He settled the star with cross and crown
And won the fair hand of the Princess Barbituary
Abigail Cleoratra
Her King from Barberry and Queen from Tuscany

Scurrying up to his arms and rat tails
In his tuxedo two tails
He grinned as coyly
As the bride exchanged vows and rings
By the solemn church priest side
All the ranting and ravings
Of the caller birds who took off
Greener pastures by migrating
Even the carnivores and herbivores
Waiters of the undergrowth
Waiting for summer to dawn again
Who settled in their underground holes
For hibernation amidst the farms and pasturage
Church and vicarage
The Wayfarers All!
And ships Ahoy!
Band of Buccaneers, crew of sea captains
A bevy of boisterous sailors and beautiful ladies
Like a bevy of famous stars of faery ferries
Till all was quiet in the valley of whispers
And murmurs of the tooth and tail
Bugles, Beagle dogs and beavers
Honey bears and monkeys
Now the guests of sea farer rat's wedding
In the galipot of blue
Turpentine the sea and sea ink

Varnished the toes of his new shy bride Abigail Cleoratra
With rings and bells on her scruff
And golden earrings for the groom
Now should they now sing a Seascrollsong
To hoist a sea flag
Or buy a new handy paintbrush......
To paint blue ink
From a turpentine Galipot!
The sea so blue
On a blue ship with masts and sails
Away his hide to the Gallipoli Peninsula!
Along with his beautiful bride Abigail Cleoratra!
On a frosted cake with circles, ribbons, icing swirls
Made of Marchpane and sprinkles of
Quins, sugar pearls and silver dragees"

Then he stopped scribbling
In his journal to pick up his paintbrush
From the ground, whistling away happily
To paint the walls that he had left unfinished
"Pra rap pree pum pa pum pheeeee......." so sweetly
Abandoning his cares in whispers, chatters and murmurs
He often spoke to himself squealing and squeaking
About his bright talents and housefly chores he yet
Had a lot to finish.... mending, painting, scrubbing
Stitching and writing poetry

Many a times felt at a loss of words to describe such
Gratifying hard work
For a few white washing splashes of lovely paint
And streaks up the ceiling
In his cosy underworld Moley End!

MR TOADY IN A HOLE

Mr Toad finally awakening from his stupor like sleep
For a moment hallucinated and dreamt that
He was in Toad Hall Mansion as cold as could be
Waking up freezing hands and feet
In his chamber calling out to the servants and maids
To carry a warm blanket
And light up the cosy toasty furnace
Then he awakened from his bright lit faery dream
To blinding reality
Feet Hands and face
All numb cold and freezing
He realised he was laced inside a burrow
Of a rabbit filled with dead twigs, bracken
Leaves and in a mess
From head to foot
Now stretching his aching arms and legs
He sprinted and began to hop
On his feet
Hoping to catch someone
Who could give him a ride home
Soon as he sauntered along the busy hedgerows
He came across the rippling waters
Of the riverside of Soda Inlet Bay
And stooped to see from afar

Under the canal bridge
A stow away burlesque mountain of a badger woman
Holding a blue dotted umbrella on a boat
He yelled to the huge burlesque Badger woman
Maybe a nanny of Frankenstein
To wait up for him
Limping with his bedraggled dress, scarf and hood
Like a toil worn ragged old wreck soggy and dripping
A freshet with heavy downpour of rains
And howling winds flooded the river
He stood looking askance at the immense boulder
Of the strange badger woman before him
And stood by the edge of the riverside
Upon his one foot in the swelling waters
Contemplating like a Ballet Stork pirouette on one leg
How to approach such a monstrous badger of a woman
As big as a washing stone stooge of comedy
He finally dragged himself and his wet dress
As he struggled through the flooded river
Pinching it high above his knees
Wading through the rushing waters
With his flowery apron and daintily bowing a curtsy
Introduced himself to the huge manly
Stow-away badger woman of the motor boat
"Hello there my dear
Would you be so kind enough to let

Me off next stop tother end
Opposite the Dahlia windmills
Dooliyaanah Toad Hall Mansion
I am a Washer-Woman
And I am used to surf and rough tide detergents
Like these on the canal trips
Could you do me a favour and help me
I have to get to my old hubby
And poor grandchildren in time"
Then he added another
"And my poor married daughter
She has no one to look after her
Since her husband went after a weasel"
Patronising her like a butter on a scone
Trying to be as kind and humble
Like a very civilized Toad Washer Woman
It didn't do much to win over her approval
And eyeing him thoroughly from head to toe
The bossy stout Badger woman
Who loved to bully animals like poor Mr Toady
Replied like a cantankerous old fossil of an immense rodent
"Well! Hmmph..... Only if you could show me
How you can wash that big
Load off my back"
And removing a bundle from her back
Displayed the contents

There were three great bed sheets
Five towels and seven pillow cases
Twenty five napkins, two uniforms and a blanket
All from a hotel she worked at
"I suppose I could if you tried to give me a chance
Sloshing err..... I mean washing"
Toady grimaced whispering to himself
"O' Dear! Good Heavens! She is a washer woman herself
What the devil have I got myself into?"
The bullish faced Badger woman soon
Suspected it was none other than
The handsome, charming
Distinguished owner of the Toad Hall Mansion
But acted as if she didn't know who he was
This she did to pun the funny creature
She showed no respect at all for the educated Mr Toady
Of Toad Hall
And said hooliganishly
"Show me if you can be a better
Washer woman than me
Only then can I oblige you
With a favour as that
Mrs Washer Woman"
Toady disgruntled and upset by her rude behaviour
And totally innocent of her suspicious nature
Accepted the onerous challenge

Then the loutish old stubborn
Bull headed woman
Removed soap, brush and a batten
To pound, scrub and wash the linen
In a bucket on the little motor boat she owned
Staring at poor Mr Toady twiddling all thumbs
He clumsily opened the soap packet
And dropped the abstergent into the bucket
The detergents started bubbling like bubbles
Blown from a bubble bottle
Circling great splatters all around poor Toady
A great big bubble bath
He began to vigorously scrub soap and use the batten to pound
But missed aim
Every time he tried scrubbing then battens
Beatings and washings
Soap got to his eyes along with big teardrops
Rolling down his cheeks
And there was soap abstergent and salt everywhere
Just like high teas and high tide detergents
Angry and viciously mad
At the scruffy old witch
To put him through such an agony
The abstergent flew in great bubbles
All around the bucket
He just couldn't get a hang at the batten

With his soapy fingers

Making poor Mr Toady even more disappointed and annoyed

Almost slipping like a dame Slip-a-lot

Head over heels

And heels over his giddy head

Totally bonkers he thought he'd turned into a fool abstergent

Handling soap studs and washing batten

To hammer the grime and dirt

Stuff called washing dirty linen in public

He was most surprised

That he was being watched all the time

By the roguish woman

Who breaking out into a spell

Of thunderously humorous claps and guffaws

Shooting daggers at him remarked insultingly

Letting out all his secrets of his skeletons in the closet

"I knew what you knew I knew already
before you knew what I knew"

Explaining to him wickedly,
humour in a gross Bumpkin manner

"You were none other than Mr Toady of Toad Hall Mansion

Not at all the washer woman you put up to be

A swell soapy act!

I swear I will put you in the lock up again

I heard that you car snatched

Your mad passion for road racing

Ho Hum! Wait till I fry your curls
And squeeze you dry
Till you cough up a good wallet of green dollars
Or else squeezy-wheezy a jail bird to be in
A Washer Woman wishy-washy prison
You should learn by now
No one in the world can beat my washing
Tide detergent skills
With my batten pounder and tub"
Mr Toad was taking none of her riff-raff chiff-chaff behaviour
And stunned her gruesomely
Waving out absurdly the batten in the air
As if to pound it on her head
He retorted angrily
"Don't you try to act smart with me
Old natty crook
I'll teach you a lesson"
Before you could say Jack Robinson
He turned the steering wheel of the motor boat
And since he was so experienced
To drive his dinghies on motor rides
The motor boat propelled out
Its horsepower outboard motor
In the riverside at full speed
He manoeuvred helm of the car motor boat
Sailing the currents at such an alarming rate

That the whole world turned topsy-turvy
The woman almost swallowed her heart in her stomach
Screaming and yelling out at Mr Toady
"Stop at once you rascal Toad
I shall have you arrested soon
Stop I say"
The boat was above the sky
And the sky turned below the sea
The boat capsized into the waters
And Mr Toady just in time
Managed to paddle his way to the river bank
Splashing and stroking his arms
From side to side he swam madly
As a quick swimmer would swimming fastly
To the river bank destination
In his washer woman garb
Then seeing a lovely young horse
Waiting right at the spot on the riverbank
Without his owner he correctly guessed belonged to the
Mountain of a Barracuda Badger Washer Woman
Mr Toady quickly sat upon it
And pulling the reigns made good his escape
Away from the shrew of a Badger washer woman
Now head to tail deep in troubled rivers
Whilst the horse began to wildly gallop
Run and then slowly began to walk

Click clocking its hooves a little mile away
Till it bowed down its young head
And began to graze in the meadows
With cow slips and honey suckles
Peeking through every nook and cranny
At last Mr Toady dismounted from the horse
And holding the horse by the rope
Started walking towards a gypsy caravan
His dress and flowery apron had dried off
The brilliant sunshine over head
He soon reached a clearing in the middle
Of the wild woods
Where sat an old beaver
A gypsy by trade
And held a faery meerschaum pipe
From which he blew out smoke
At intervals like magical puff rings over
Mr Toady the frantic washer woman
Wishing to be in his cosy mansion once again
Pulling himself together decided to ask
The old gypsy beaver for some help
He had a huge pot bubbling
Over a fire wood
And the smell that arose from it
Was so delicious
Filling the empty spaces of the butterflies

In weary old Mr Toady's hungry stomach
He had to taste some of the melting magic pot stew
And so he sat near the old gypsy Beaver
Hoping to chat him up
"O' dear" said Mr Toad
"So much of work to do for a poor washer woman
Work for my old Husband
My grandchildren
And my poor married daughter
She has no one for her
You know
Since her husband went after a weasel"
The gypsy had no expression
On his chubby face
Tweaking his whiskers he said
"What if you sell that young horse?
Washer Woman
One dollar a leg and a hoof
For that youthful beast
I would offer"
Mr Toady thought and resolved
There would be no better bargain
Than this
Then wrangling he went on
"Only four dollars for four legs and four hooves
I'd make it six dollars and four cents

If your answer is no
I'll save it for my customer I am acquainted with
Who lives right at the
Wendan by the curve of the forest
He would offer me at least ten dollars
For that youthful dreamy mare"
Mr Toad invented it all in his wise old head
For he hadn't even a cent in his pockets
This was the only way to earn a few dimes and dollars
The gypsy beaver went inside his
Tent and brought out the money
Then turning it into Mr Toady's
Hands
He sulked and said to toad
"I couldn't afford it really
That type of money
To make would take a whole month
We gypsies are fond of horse-trading
Well anyway this is all I could offer you?
And some of my broth too"
Toady couldn't be happier
Than words could express
To the kind old soul and his soul pot
The old gypsy beaver
Returned to his caravan tent
And fetched from inside

A large bowl with a silver spoon
Then pouring the magic broth
Into it
Mr Toady smelt rabbits, pheasants
Turkeys, cows, geese, pigs
Duck, partridge, pigeon, Mutton and lamb
All brewing up his magical cauldron pot
On the stout handle
At the very top
Of a fire wood
After a warm bowl of scrumptious broth in the humble dwelling
In the midst of the blundering thicket
He squalled like a baby
And wept like a toad
Tears for joy
Then waved the gypsy Beaver a good bye
He composed a ditty on Mr Toady the great
And his peril's

"MR TOADY THE GREAT"

Mr Toady the great
In all of history books
His spate of adventures
To relate

Would definitely be a crime!
Faery tale, fiction or fantasy
You decide
From his primitive life
At the Toad Hall Mansion
Dated Seventeen Sixty Five
His Great Great Great Grand Uncle
Mr Dooliyaanah Little Toad of
Dooliyaanah Mansion
And all the doodahlings Queens and Kings
Countesses and Counts Vampire Toad Dragons
Of long before
And his darling Vampire Toad Countessa bride to be
Sugar plum Dotty Grimmwauld in the present world
Even through grim circumstance
He'd learnt to profess true love
And date with fangs
A flick with slick oil tongues bottleneck wasps
Spur throated Flies of Cowboys called Buzz of Buzzybods
Razzle-dazzle bugs called Hums of Humbugs
And a strange case swarm of Hollywood Bees Buzzub Buzzub Beezeeb
Hard to swallow........
Family of buzzers and hummers we call flies and family ties
Good Riddance to all Hogwashing Ballyhoo water sloshing
Now passing history through

Oxford University
The dignified and distinguished
Student Pupil well extinguished Mr Toad
Had fallen love at first sight
With a Baron's daughter
Now through hard crimes
You'd fine easy to define
Car snatching
Road rages
Racing and hammering
Smashing, swinging, belabouring
With washing battens
He emerged Victorious Knight
Hounded, grounded even pounded
By police men
Detectives, gaolers, foxes, dogs and cats
The stiff and bleak
Story of Mr Toady
The learned and distinguished man
Now through surf and tide detergents
Through rivers and boats
Catamarans he owned by dozens
He made his way
In history of Oxford Dictionary of Oxford Great Britain
And through pages flipped American Encyclopaedia
Mr Toad from family Bufonidae

The brave and dignified
The riff-raff even chiff-chaff
The simple yet complicated
He put on a swell soap act
The polished washer woman
The smart and sometimes petrified
Bold Gold Daring Mr Toad and his perils
Hurrah! Yippee! Yahooo!

Further after blabbering
His proud stanza on bold Mr Toad
In his good books as good as glittering gold
He found out he was soon just a kilometre away
From Dooliyaanah Mansion
As he neared the path along the fringe lip of the highway
He recognised the Blue Whale Inn
The same spot he car snatched
And Limshinnybodkins!
He caught sight of the same handsome
Buggy gaining speed by his side
Mr Toady started sweating and worrying

"O' dear soon these creatures
Will recognise the car snatcher
Prison breaker
Chased by police dogs

Dodged by trains
Hounded, pounded and grounded
By magnifying glasses of detectives
Guns, revolvers and truncheons
Woe begone! I shall have to live
In the squalid dungeon of a hole
And live on water and dry bread
Save me! Save my soul"
He whimpered and he cried to himself
But all was not lost
Till the owners mistook his identity
As the simpleton washer woman
Not the strikingly dashing Django Mr Toady of Toad Hall Mansion
Who one day had car snatched their handsome car
Had had him arrested and imprisoned in a gaol
But now mistaking Toady as the little washer woman
Trudge slowly along the sunshine path
They thought was a poor thing
Deserving to be given a good ride
To her work place
And calling out to her they said
"Wait up you poor thing
We could drop you if you wish
To wherever you would like to be dropped
Come with us"

And made her sit right next to the driver's seat
A temptation poor Toady could hardly resist again
Then speaking hap haply winking to her
Chivalrous saviours
She said;
"I've half a half baked idea
To sit in the seat if you wouldn't mind
And drive you
You'd be surprised how it would turn
Your ride a ride you'd never want to ever forget
A race driver like me"
Chiding he said
"A Poor Little Washer Woman!"
Remembering their revenge of making
Mr Toady suffer in the gruesome jail
Like a Jailbird
He donned Toad wings to avenge with spite
To cap good ounce of humour tightly and squeeze
A good throttle over necks and engines
The good old phrase
'REVENGE IS BITTERSWEET!'
'REVENGE IS BITTERSWEET INDEED!'
As they unknowingly fell into his smooth honey trap
Of a slick slimy oily tongue and soon were
Flicked inside it like flies to a honey pot!
Whence fore like his obedient passengers

Allowed him to take care of the steer wheel
Quiet fancying how a washer woman could handle
To drive them from a bubble in a dream
That turned to a skittish nightmare
They never wished to experience their whole blighted lives
However managed to escape through a brush with a game of nine skittles
Race and war you could say over Toady's brushes with law
A skirmish that existed betwixt
Two stoats a weasel and a toad from Toad's Addams!
All over a handsome car~
At first Mr Toady drove like a normal bean
And they were surprised at a Washer Woman's skill at driving
But then he swerved the wheel
AND WHOOOSH.......
Off he raced the car deep into the wild woods
Screaming at his wrong doers
"It was me all the time
Bold and brazen Mr Toady of Toad Hall Mansion
The replica reincarnation
Of Mr Dooliyaanah Little Toad
My Great Great Great Grand Vampire Toad of an Uncle"
Far from the police, from the gaoler
The bullish washer woman who wished to gaol him again
The kind soul gypsy beaver
And the golden Buttercup faery ferret little Gretel

He was thoroughly enjoying his car ride
With his guests inside slurring out vindictive oaths
And promises
He would regret
When suddenly the unexpected took place
And the car swerved into the tall bull rush pond
By the Toad Hills and Toadstools
With all the creatures it carried
The wheels were totally flown in the sky
Along with the tires burnt to carbon
The owner's two stoats and a weasel
Waving and flailing their hands wildly
At Mr Toady from their plunge inside a shallow pond
Mr Toady jumping through the window
Running, sprinting and hopping as fast as he could
Spotted a Toad in the hole
A hole big enough to let him inside
Muddy and dark filled with water
Just sufficient he slithered and slid
Into its open hole and swam right at the edge
Then saw a little face wriggle from below
As brown and black as a coal
Sleek and shiny coat of moonshine whiskers and fur
"It couldn't be the water rat
Mr Water Ratty..... Would it?"
Toadie wondered hoping it was really true

"Yes" bubbled a voice from below the pond
Inside the water rat or toad hole
"It's me"
Affirmed Water Ratty to poor little rich and happy Mr Toad
And pulling him by the scruff of his neck
Mr Water Ratty brought Mr Toady
To the edge of the bank
From his water rat hole end
Where he lived

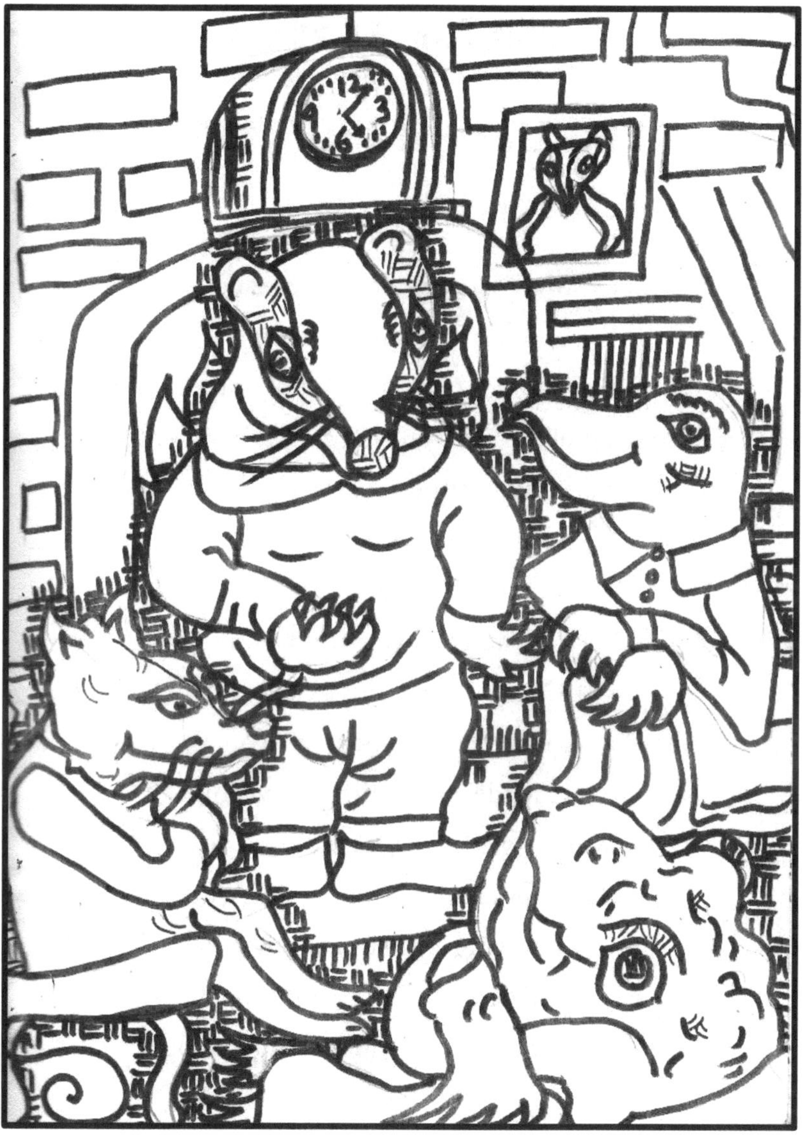

THE WILD WOOD CREATURES AND THE SLY FOXES

TEARS LIKE A SUMMER TEMPEST!

Mr Water Ratty then took poor
Mr Toady inside his neat and
Well furnished rat hole
After lugging him out through the water rat hole
Like a bulky portmanteau of a washer woman
Soaked and washed rolling on its wheels
That he had slipped into
After a good cry
And good many a hugs
Over a cup of hot ginger tea
And delicious blueberry scones
He made Toady first change his
Washer woman attire into one of his
Crisp pyjama's and carpet flip flops
Removing and hooking the old
Wet dress, hood, mittens
Scarf and apron upon the clothes hanger
Mr Toady related to him
How like a Vampire Toad
He spent his three months
Languishing in a dungeon cell

As bleak as a black hole
And then recounted his strange adventures
".......And with the help
Of a blonde ferret of
A young maiden
The helpful and wise daughter
Of the gaoler
Pretty Darling little Gretel
I took a bold risk
Escaping my prison sentence much in advance
Encountering the horrid
Legion of police, detectives
Hounds, bugles, truncheons
Revolvers and pistols
Even through the train tunnel, rough roads
Of the deep wild woods
Its Forest filled with sly foxes and
The querulous badger woman
The kind old gypsy Beaver
My rides once again in a boat
On a young horse and the same handsome
Car I car snatched"
He yelped a mad bark in frenzy
Of excitement as he continued
To retell his great adventure
"And the strange water logged burrow

Where at last I hid after assuming
The character of the washer woman
In her tatty long dress, flowery apron
Hood, mittens and scarf
Here I am Mr Ratty home at last"

Mr Water Ratty however looked
Worried and fretted
But before Mr Water Ratty let out the sorry
Secret of the Wild Wood Creatures
The Sly foxes and their mischief
He hesitated
As Mr Toad looked so happy
Wishing to spend the rest of his
Days not like the foolish toad he once was
After he confessed to Mr Water Ratty
"I have changed Water Ratty my friend
For the better
Now none of those car racing fevers
Or car snatching bouts do I suffer from
I've learnt to handle tough situations
And hope to outshine like my
Great Great Great Grand Uncle
Mr Dooliyaanah Little Toad
Carrying his torch as a beacon of light
To all my friends of the wild woods"

Water Ratty didn't want to shy
From what he had to say to Mr Toad
And patting Mr Toady on his back
For his beautiful transformation
He brought out the grim matter
Before him
"Mr Toady Alas! Alls not well
As it may seem here in Dooliyaanah Mansion
The wild wood creatures some of them
Began to blame you for their misfortunes
And said it was a good thing Mr Toad
Has to learn a lesson
He always set a bad example
Squandering away the wealth of his
Great Great Great Grand Uncle
And all of the stoats, beavers, ferrets, weasel
And rest of the few sly foxes
In fact most untrusting few members of the wild wood
Who had an eye on Dooliyaanah mansion
Decided to camp there
After all finally lay siege to your fortress
It was of no use for us three friends
To confront those conniving crooks
Fifty or seventy of them against us
They sent us all flying away with battens
And their rifles as they shot curses in the air

Blaming you and saying
Dooliyaanah masion is ours now and was
So from the very day Mr Toad was in prison
As we all had suspected with these
Conjuring foxes, vixen, stoats, ferrets
And weasels
One bad fruit spoils the others
Envy, jealousy and covetousness
Festering inside their black hearts"
Mr Toady croaked and cried so much after hearing
The sad story
Almost tears as big and unpredictable
As the summer's Tempest
"A mid-summers horrible nightmare"
He sighed in misery

Mr Water Ratty enveloped his arms lovingly
Around the poor extinguished
Mr Toad with always a fiery spark
Of enthusiasm smouldering away
In his red Vampire Eyes
He knew he had a fascination for Vampires
And even had assumed his
Faery mansion Dooliyaanah
Possessed a secret tunnel
And a secret trap door to enter inside it
That his dear Great Great Great Grand

Uncle Mr Dooliyaanah Little Toad
Had fully stocked with food
Rations, arms and ammunition
A secret passage hideaway with a
Bomb proof bunker fully made of steel and iron
Nobody had ever known about
He had it in a scroll map showing its exact location
Which he always kept hidden
In one of his bedroom chambers
Though never had tried himself to discover it
He went on to say:
'Till the two headed hammer became one'
The symbol encrypted on it
Which read:
"It shall pave path for immortalizing
Great Great Great Grand Uncle
Mr Dooliyaanah Little Toad
The two headed hammer used for
Destruction, protection and fertilization
On the Mountain of Mars
Linking destiny by a battlefield of bloodshed
Even if it meant violence for obtaining its
Title of honour and rightfully possession
Of property as a symbol of sacrificial inversion
And manual labour to light a torch in darkness"

Then having the ball in his court
Mr Toady emphasized what he had to say
Were valuable words of wisdom worth
500 thousand bucks supposed to sit like
A white elephant in a museum withstanding
Moral decay through a fast moving space travel time machine
And something was needed to be done in order to put
The two headed hammer symbol the scroll map depicted
Into action to unravel its ancient wisdom
And obtain his rightful title and possession back
That the brilliant Vampire Great Great Great Grand Toad
In his Dooliyaanah Mansion Museum legacy
Left behind his heirs to accomplish.....
The colourful story of a bear eating the bull
In a vicious battle and winning title
As well as immortalizing the King
That he explained put together all pieces of a great puzzle
That is why he felt his Great Great Great
Grand Uncle was so much like
A Vampire Toad
If only he could show his fangs
To those crooked officers stoats
Grimy weasels, camouflage lizards
And the snarling chef of police Hound Baskerville
Who made his life hellish
At the misery gaol

He concluded to Mr Water Ratty

"Victory is ours to Conquer"

And began singing the beautiful song

He opened from Mr Water Ratty's parish hymnal book

Of his neat little library

Ceremoniously flipping through the middle pages

Of the little hymnal......Pg 207

......Pg 207

The Victory is Ours

By Davis

Verse 1

There is a war going on in the heavenlies
Between the powers of darkness and light
But through our worship we will be victorious
His Word has promised that we win the fight

Chorus 1

Put your foot on the head of the devil
Clap your hands lift a triumphant shout
Greater is He that's living within us
The victory is ours!

Verse 2

Faith is our shield
Our breastplate is righteousness
The Word of God our two edged sword
We're clothed in power that renders hell powerless
We overcome through the name of the Lord

Bridge

Put your foot on the head of the devil
Clap your hands lift a triumphant shout
Greater is He that's living within us
The victory is ours!
Victory victory
Through Jesus name we have victory!!
Victory victory

Through Jesus name we have victory!! 8X

Chorus 2

Put your foot on the head of the devil

Clap your hands lift a triumphant shout

Greater is He that's living within us

Ending

The victory is ours!

The victory is ours!

Hallelujah!

The victory is ours!

Then he added with a fiery spark in his eyes
"My dear friend Water Ratty
I do hope Mr Badger and Mr Moley
Come up with some honourable solutions
Or I shall have to use powers
That goes beyond reasoning
Of my ancient
Great Great Great Grand Vampire Toad
Mr Dooliyaanah Little Toad's secret magic tunnel way
To lead us inside this depravity
Of being possessed by demonic wild wood creatures
And sly vixens and foxes
Hoping to cure their evil propensities
By thinking they own the mansion themselves
Prophesy or a curse with my crystal ball of luck

A spell to cast for them by me
With my wretched fangs
Rrrrrrr Rippet Rrrrrrr"
And he opened wide his mouth
Snarling and swearing below his breath
To show those fangs at last that frightened
Poor Mr Moley who had already arrived
Just in time Water Ratty's hole-end
To give them company
Raising hairs on his fur coat and
Giving him Goosebumps all over
Terrified him to the very core
There were four shiny fangs
Right at each side of his malevolent grin
Up and down his blood curdling mouth
As he never did reform 'A humorous bone'
He always had them from childhood
And was proud of his sharpened fangs
To go with witty repartee
A quick mind as well his splendid gift of gab
Like a reincarnation of reformed
Mr Dooliyaanah Little Toady

Soon there was a knock on the door
Mr Water Ratty knew Mr Badger had arrived
Mr Badger dumbstruck

Upon seeing the appearance of Mr Toady he didn't
Believe was true at first or imagined it was a ghost......
Christmas Ghost of a Christmas Carol
Of Great Great Great Grand Mr Dooliyaanah Little Toad
Come into sight before his wide popping eyes
And rubbing them vigorously as if in a dream
He pinched himself and cried out ecstatically
"It's Mr Toady"
Mr Toady shrieked back at him
"O' DEAR DEAR Mr Badger
I'm HOME HOME AT LAST!
For all my shenanigans and mischief
Forgive me all my dear friends"
They cuddling the crook
Exchanging their warm kind
Verbal joy of squeals, shrills,
Whistles and vigorous hand shake
Physical tremors
And quakes of cuddles again and again
Of happy reunion
They heard the full story right from the beginning
Mr Badger as well as Mr Moley
Holding on to their breath
Heard everything Mr Toady had to say
All about the secret passage leading to the mansion
The secret trap door

Whilst Mr Badger made himself comfortable
In his simple slacks, blue gumboots and over coat
And sat down on the armchair
In serious contemplation
Removing his newspaper and huge spectacles
To read through it and
The Headlines **'MR TOADY ESCAPES'**
Thinking seriously at the same time
How were they going to fight four against so many
Vicious Hooligans and Conniving Hoodlums
Whilst Mr Moley made deductions
Hoping to come out with some
Superb idea and after seeing the natty
Fancy dress of the washer woman hanging on the door
He came up with one brilliant
Solution to the problem
In his head like a light bulb flash all at once
Without containing himself spilled it out
His conniving plan to outwit the wrongdoers
Dressed up in Mr Toady's washer woman outfit
Sneaking up to steal Mr Toady's Great
Great Great Grand Uncle's
Secret 'Two Headed Hammer' map of the
underground hidden tunnel
The only way to enter the Dooliyaanah Mansion
That he quickly hammered out a speech to his friends

Like Speedy Gonzales a famous cowboy rat song

He first sang------

It was a moonlit night in old Mexico

I walked alone between some old adobe haciendas

Suddenly, I heard the plaintive cry of a young Mexican Rat girl

You better come home, Speedy Gonzales

Away from tannery row

Stop all a your a-drinkin'

With that floozy named Flo

Come on home to your adobe

And slap some mud on the wall

The roof is leakin' like a strainer

There's loads a roaches in the hall

Speedy Gonzales (Speedy Gonzales)

Why don't cha come home?

Speedy Gonzales (Speedy Gonzales)

How come ya leave me all alone?

"Hey, Rosita, I have to go shopping downtown for my mother

She needs some tortillas and chili peppers"

Your doggy's gonna have a puppy

And we're runnin' outta Coke

No enchiladas in the icebox

And the television's broke

I saw some lipstick on your sweatshirt

I smelled some perfume in your ear
Well if you're gonna keep on messin'
Don't bring your business back a-here
Mmm, Speedy Gonzales (Speedy Gonzales)
Why don't cha come home?
Speedy Gonzales (Speedy Gonzales)
How come ya leave me all alone?
"Hey, Rosita come quick
Down at the cantina they giving green stamps with tequila"

Caught in the heat of the moment pepped up
With excitement and passion after singing the ranger
Or rancher rat cowboy song
Mr Moley like a busybody mole of a meddlesome actor Ratboy
Animating his great master plan with a gunshot and a
Blow of breath off his make believe pistol
Started to talk the well devised agenda
To play role of four stooges of slapstick comedy
As a Washer woman and his friends Mr Badger
Mr Toad and Mr Water Ratty following close behind
"The very next morning
As early as the crows wake up....
I shall dress up as the washer woman
That Mr Toad dressed up as in the first place
Whilst you follow behind me"

Then pointing to the costume of the washer woman
Hanging from the hooks on the clothes hanger
He continued to explain to his friends
Who listened rapt all ears
"Then knock on the door of the Toad Hall Mansion
Telling them there
About the rumour that all the wild wood creatures
Along with Toady had a master plan
To seize the Dooliyaanah Mansion once again
The few handful sly wild wood creatures
That illegally camped over there
Would be shocked and stupefied at the outcome
Of my plan
For I am going to traumatize them out their blooming wits
Till they fry in a pan
Tremble and quiver
Shake in their pants
Saying that Mr Toady has Fifty toads
Fifty moles, fifty badgers and fifty
Stoats, weasels, ferrets, mice
In an army to beat you all at once
Be prepared.....Do or die!
At the same time I'd steal the secret map
From Mr Toady's master Bedroom
The one which Toady said
Had the route of the hidden

Underground tunnel
To the Dooliyaanah mansion Trap-door!"

Mr Moley was hundred percent sure
This rumour he made up
Would rattle them up like a poisonous venom
Whilst the rotten scoundrels let him
Take care of the job dressed as a common washer woman
Come to wash their dirty linen
Would shake them to their roots and foundation
Make them tremble at their knees
And buckle them
Up for war
Then late at night they could take the enroute
With many of the devoted and helpful creatures
Of the wild woods
With the help of the stolen map
Of the hidden underground tunnel
Armed with all their weapons and those stashed away in
His Great Great Great Grand Uncle's secret
Hideaway passage
Mr Badger, Mr Water Ratty, Mr Moley and Mr Toady
Chinked their glasses together
And chorused together
Joining one foot of a rat, toad, mole and badger
Like a lucky Pirate Rat Ratatouille's footprints ring of charm

That they invented in one of their wild wood games
Inside a magic ring of faery mushrooms
"Here to our magic footprints good luck charm!
And Mr Moley's encounter with the sly foxes
The badgers, vixen, stoats, weasels
Ferrets and mice
As a commoner Moley washer woman
To steal our treasured map of the hidden tunnel"
"Boo! Doom and Gloom!
To those unlucky scoundrels
Who betrayed you their dear friend Mr Toad"
Mr Moley ended the conversation
And the four thick as thieves best friends
Had a good night's rest in Mr Water Ratty's hole-end
Soon morning dawned
The sparrows twittered up the Whispering
Willow trees
The crows lit the sky like a match
Like a tinder strikes
With their caw-caws and chak-chaks
Mr Moley as planned
Dressed up in Mr Toady's
Washer woman dress and flowery apron
With a black hood, black mittens
And the colourful scarf
Set out on his foreboding mission

Whilst Mr Badger, Mr Toady and Mr Water Ratty
Followed closely behind him
Enacting the four comic stooges of Slapstick comedy
Hiding among the thickets
Set to light the Toad Hall Mansion on fire
Mr Moley made his way
To the steps of Dooliyaanah Mansion
As stout hearted as ever
Anything would he do
For his dear friend Mr Toad

Ringing the door bell
With the same pleasant
'Brriiiing Brrraaang Brrriiing'
Only now knowing well
The eerie dangerous creatures who thought
They owned the dear mansion of Mr Toad forever
And refused to budge out
Made him jittery and sent a shiver tingling through his spine
But hoping dearly not to miss this excellent
Opportunity to get the secret map
Of the hidden passage
Mr Moley put on a swell act
Whilst Mr Badger and Mr Moley watched
From afar inside the hidden bushes
Mr Moley told the dumb

Believing stoat who attended the door
"It's me a washer woman
Any dirty linen to wash?
I do all laundry and ironing
And even secrets of dirty linen I wash"
He led her to inside the silenced
Haunting mansion
Mr Moley knew the way right through and happily
Took the staircase to Mr Toady's
Master bedroom
There was a bathroom there
And the secret map inside his drawer
In the stupid stoat's absence she closed the door behind
Him and secretly rejoiced
Opening the drawer and robbing
Mr Toady's Great Great Great Grand Uncle
Little Dooliyaanah's precious map
Then putting it inside her large apron pockets
Made a washing and wringing
Noise inside the bathroom
Beating with washing batten the dirty linen
That the dumb stoat had handed to her
Pouring and splashing out buckets of water
She put the soggy clothes back inside
The bucket
And came trip-tropping down the stairway

To hang the laundry out to dry on the line
Then before she could leave
She commented to one of the high and dry
Mean and mighty foxes and ferrets
Riding on their high horses
Also to one of the weasel and sly vixen
Washing out their ears with
The rumour she fooled she had heard about
Mr Moley went on to say to the scoundrels
Hoping to shock them like a bunch of Shocking Pansies
And back off like those blooming Violet Shies
Those Mr Wiley Niley's
As if she was proudly showing off to them
"I heard the rumour that Mr Toady has fifty toads
Fifty moles, fifty badgers and fifty
Stoats, weasels, ferrets, mice
In an army in order to beat you all at once
And reclaim Toad Hall Mansion back again
Be prepared
Do or die
Good Luck to you my friends!"
Then swaying hips like a fidgety
Old natter jack mole washer woman of
Impersonation she left the Toad Hall Mansion
Turning a mole into a mountain!
Or paving a mole hill out of a mountain!

For the four comic stooges of slapstick comedy
A mountain of a Mole hill indeed to start off with
Their next march through the Dooliyaanah tunnel of course!

VICTORY IN DOOLIYAANAH MANSION
THROUGH THE SECRET PASSAGE
RETURN OF ULYSSES VAMPIRE MR TOAD
LITTLE DOOLIYAANAH

As soon as Mr Moley joined Mr Badger, Mr Water
Ratty and Mr Toady
They quietly made their way through the leering
And back towards Mr Water Ratty's hole-end
Whilst on their way out
They heard a buzz and murmur of voices
As if the bad eggs were scared to the core
By the rumour they all witnessed to hear
And were half their minds to run far away
From The Dooliyaanah Mansion
So the three friends secretly watched and waited
From afar the lights still shone inside the mansion
The intruders weren't going to vacate the place
Or give up so soon
War and Victory
Do or Die!
Was on the mind of Mr Toad, Mr Badger
Mr Water Ratty and the sly foxes,
Vixens, stoats, ferrets, mice, weasels
Who had strayed from their
Path and took to conquer

The Great Great Great Grand Vampire's
Empire till it was the return
Of the Ulysses Vampire Toad Little Dooliyaanah!
The secret of the two headed hammer
That was going to be unravelled to pave way for them
To defeat the Nemesis and hail victory
Till the two headed hammer became one!

The rest trusted creatures
Of the wild woods assembled together
For a meeting somewhere
Deep in heart of a cave
Mr Badger's fifty badgers
Mr Moley's fifty moles
Mr Water Ratty's fifty water rats
And Mr Toady's fifty Vampire Toads
Along with fifty a few many good honest
Stoats, weasels, ferrets, field mice
Beavers and rabbits
All in the heart of the cove
Where Mr Toady confessed to his dear friends
He had acted like a rash, immature
Impractical and stupid creature
But now he was changed
And would henceforth put his money to better use
For reforms in the forest and uplifting the downtrodden

He would implement some handy
Plans like housing, comfortable prison cells
And horse trader gypsies to look after his horses and farms
Even washer women would have jobs
At the mansions of all his uppity class friends
Of the wild woods
Which after their mortal Kombat
He would put into action
The army of woodland creatures happy with what was said
Cheered for Mr Toady their dear rich and benevolent friend
Whispering and murmuring
Amongst themselves
"Hurrah Hurrah
Our Mr Toad of Dooliyaanah
Will win back his mansion again
Return Of the Ulysses Vampire Toad Little Dooliyaanah!
And Its Two Headed Hammer
Hurrah! Hurrah!"
Soon Mr Toad opened the scroll
Of the secret map
The two headed Hammer
Pointed to an opening in the ground
Near the Whispering Willow Tree
To the west of the courtyard
To understand this concept just consider
One motion which is earth's spin on its axis

Hot warm not in the least a cold dead end
In search of a hot and cold game
'The sun rises in the east and sets in the west'
An optimist with his cup full would never stray
From his path finding its treasured spot down below a hole
As one who believeth in God is seldom left guessing
His true path to perfection and to the Gates of Heaven
For all righteous
As the wondrous beatitudes on their pilgrim journey
There was a secret hatch door and a
Passageway to a hidden tunnel
That led the way right up
To the Dooliyaanah Mansion
They creatures of the wild woods brought out
All the arms and ammunition
They possessed and stacked them
Up in a neat pile
Then using belts
They hung all their weapons from a hook
A truncheon, cutlass, revolver,
Even maybe a rifle, spear, stick or a pistol
And decided to set out to the secret passage
In the middle of night
Till then they briefed all the rest
Those without ammunition would be armed
With weapons they found inside the

Hidden tunnel which was supposed
To be stacked fully with equipment
And ammunitions
Soon time ticked by quickly
And the owls began to hootenanny
"Twu Whit Twhu Whoots
It's two AM
And the wild wood seems so dead
I would like to go to bed
Better be prudent what lies ahead
Twu Whit Twhu Whoots"
Then they quietly and stealthily
Began to march their way
Through the deafening silence of the dense thicket
And towards the Whispering Willow Tree
To the west of the courtyard
Of Dooliyaanah Masion
On tip toes TRIP TROP TRIPPET TRIP TROP
They marched
Once Mr Toady behind
Mr Badger surprised him
With a nudge
Mr Badger was so unnerved and thought
They were being attacked from behind
He was ready to put the bullet
Right through Mr Toady's poor head

"Silence" he told Mr Toad
And warned the others
"Any disturbance now
From you or anybody else
Will not be allowed in with us"
Mr Toad was shaken up so badly
That he made no sound
And marched behind his friends
And the faithful soldiers behind him
The trustworthy creatures of the wild wood
One by one they dropped into
The hole of the secret tunnel
As they opened the latch above it
Saw that the great tunnel below
Was filled with lamps overhead
Which they lit up with their fire sticks
Like torch lamps of a marathon race
And each who hadn't any weapons
Collected the equipment stashed
Away in its nooks and crannies
At first was dark as a dungeon hole
But with the torch lights lit up
Revealed marvellously clean
And beautifully built bomb proof bunkers
Without a single flaw
It had steel bed bunks, tables and chairs

Which Great Great Great Grand
Uncle Dooliyaanah Little Toad
Had taken great pains and measures
In making perfect to the point of Iron Grit
Iron fangs and steely gauntlets
Of an Iron Vampire Toad Knight's Iron bunker!
Made fully of solid iron and steels
In case of floods or any sort
Of battles that would
Evolve as if he predicted in
Advance the enemies
The sly foxes and beavers
Stoats and ferrets....
All intruders who had occupied
Dooliyaanah Mansion illegally
And with their burning lamps lit with
Fire and tinder matches
Soon made their way
Through the endless tunnel
Finally reaching the spot
At tother end of the narrow long tunnel
Then lifted each another
Shoulder to shoulder
To enter into the
Dooliyaanah masion
First it was Mr Badger

Then Mr Moley
Then Mr Water Ratty
And then Mr Toady
And last but not the least
Were the remaining innocent creatures
Of the woodland
Stoats, weasels, badgers, hares
Rabbits, ferrets, meeces, moles,
Water rats and Vampire Toads
In great numbers
All armed with their weapons and equipments
And those they found inside the secret tunnel
For some who hadn't any
Now hung from their belts
And lifting up their battens
From their hooks to pound crooks
They were already in the dark wine cellar
Of the Castle of the Count Toad
Soon they heard noises
Of feet pattering
Down the steps
It was the sly fox
Come to take one of Mr Toady's fine Bourbon Whiskeys
Armed with a rifle
However upon seeing the army of soldiers
In the lamp lit cellar

He panicked and before he could
Make good his way out
He was given a sound pounding
On his head till he lay numb and senseless
They marched upstairs
Knowing the sly foxes, beavers
Stoats, vixens, ferrets, meeces
And others who captured the place
Would be armed and dangerous
Though they shivered
And were on tenterhooks mustered up courage
To face the crooks bravely and smartly
Outdo them and send them out packing
Their lugs and luggages
Bags and hammages
Making right the damages
They were resolute firm and optimistic
For they were many against the seventy
Crooks in Dooliyaanah Mansion
To carry forth the Two headed Hammer Mission X 1
Whilst their deadly rivals
Those conniving foes, vixen, stoats, ferrets, mice and sly foxes
Had purposely put out lights of the mansion
In order to befuddle them
Waiting in the dark to pounce
Upon the stout hearted soldiers

But they really didn't know what happened
In the pitch black room of the hallways and staircases
With sticks and stones
With rifles and shots
With pummels and smashing
Swinging and belabouring
Victory on its way
Mr Toady and his avenger battalion
Shook the seventy crooks asunder
Without hurting a single hair on their heads
For they made out the scoundrels at once
As all of Mr Toady's soldiers had worn
Neon Vampire Bat masques
In order to distinguish themselves from the rest
Like a masquerade soldier battalion
Whose smart thinking was by Toady himself
Suggesting such a splendid idea as that
They flickered in the dark
Like dancing fire flies
Exultantly singing the team anthems
Whilst swinging their maces and
Clobbers, shots from rifles and revolvers
Pistols and guns, spears, cutlasses and daggers
From their holsters and belts
At last the remaining nasty creatures I mean the enemies
Packed themselves out for a good run

Through the courtyard and back into
The wild woods never to be seen
Again Mr Toad was victorious
And sang a jubilant song of Victory

"RETURN OF ULYSSES VICTORY"

"Toady of Toad Hall Dooliyaanah Mansion
With all my vampire army
I have won! I have won!
At last the battle
Return of the Ulysses Vampire Toad Little Dooliyaanah!
Through my Great Great Great Grand
Uncle Dooliyaanah Little Toady's Mystery tunnel
And trap door
I've Won! I've Won! I've Won!
With our neon bat masques and masquerade party of Kombat soldiers
Now to the doors from pillar to post
And church bells on top of belfries
Surmounting all obstacles and hurdles
To span and delve the mystery of the two headed hammer X 1
That Great Great Great Grand Uncle Dooliyaanah Little Toad
Hammered and pound
Will I go forth now bravely bold and brashly
But shining like a diamond in the rough

A steely Vampire Knight Toad
To meet my love
Pulling an ace up my sleeve
To show all my love cards of hearts at once!
Before my Vampire Toadess
Lovelorn Dotty Grimmwauld
Who waited so sadly
And faithfully for me
All these years of Woe Begone! Misery
Now I shall have her hand
In marriage at last
Daughter of the Baron and Baroness
And Countess bride
Of Count Toad of Dooliyaanah
Toad Hall Mansion
Fetching her like a Toad Prince
Her holy sceptre and golden globe ball!
Under moonshine and panoply of silver stars!
Making her dreams come true at last!
And the two headed hammer becomes one!
Rippet Rippet Rippet Croak Croak!
RETURN OF ULYSSES VICTORY"

"Hurrah! Hurrah!" Cheered
Good old Badger, Water Ratty, Moley
And rest of the Vampire Bat soldiers of

The wild wood critters
With their masques and masquerade
In the magical mystical woods of the
Whispering Willows!

THE
HAPPY END
COUNT TOAD
COUNTESS TOADESS

Few points to ponder
Those wonder words of wisdom yonder
Like old is treasured gold
Where whispering willows behold
Secrets of wild woods unfold
The magical hour
That the golden globe brings into power

**DEEP BLUE SEA
IN THE LAND OF MAGIC
YOU BRING PEACE AND LOVE
YOU SHINE STARS AND PLANETS
IN YOUR REFLECTING WAVES OF SHEEN
AND SHIMMERY GLOSS
DEEP BLUE SEA
IN THE LAND OF MAGIC
OVER THE HORIZON
MY BOAT SAILS YON'
TO REACH THE ISLES OF EIGHT BEATITUDES
WHERE THE LORD SHALL BLESS EACH ONE
HOPING TO WIN OUR LOSSES WITH GLADNESS
AND SAIL WITH OUR OARS BACK TO THE LAND
OF MAGIC AS WE REMEMBER
NOT ONE FORGOT BY THE NAME OF OUR LORD
AND SAVIOUR JESUS CHRIST!**

When Adam delved, and Eve span, who was then the gentleman? From the beginning all men by nature were created alike, and our bondage or servitude came in by the unjust oppression of naughty men. For if God would have had any bondmen from the beginning, he would have appointed who should be bond, and who free. And therefore I exhort you to consider that now the time is come, appointed to us by God, in which ye may (if ye will) cast off the yoke of bondage, and recover liberty. John Ball

The solemn blessings (*beatitudines, benedictiones*) which mark the opening of the Sermon on the Mount, the very first of Our Lord's sermons in the Gospel of St. Matthew (5:3-10).

The text of St. Matthew runs as follows:

Blessed are the poor in spirit: for theirs is the kingdom of heaven. (*Verse 3*)

Blessed are the meek: for they shall possess the land. (*Verse 4*)

Blessed are they who mourn: for they shall be comforted. (*Verse 5*)

Blessed are they that hunger and thirst after justice: for they shall have their fill. (*Verse 6*)

Blessed are the merciful: for they shall obtain mercy. (*Verse 7*)

Blessed are the clean of heart: for they shall see God. (*Verse 8*)

Blessed are the peacemakers: for they shall be called the children of God. (*Verse 9*)

Blessed are they that suffer persecution for justice' sake, for theirs is the kingdom of heaven. (*Verse 10*)

THE END